English for Academic Research

Series Editor
Adrian Wallwork, English for Academics SAS
Pisa, Italy

This series aims to help non-native, English-speaking researchers communicate in English. The books are designed like manuals or user guides to help readers find relevant information quickly, and assimilate it rapidly and effectively.

More information about this series at https://link.springer.com/bookseries/13913

Adrian Wallwork

Giving an Academic Presentation in English

Intermediate Level

Springer

Adrian Wallwork
English for Academics
Pisa, Italy

ISSN 2625-3445   ISSN 2625-3453   (electronic)
English for Academic Research
ISBN 978-3-030-95608-0   ISBN 978-3-030-95609-7   (eBook)
https://doi.org/10.1007/978-3-030-95609-7

© The Editor(s) (if applicable) and The Author(s), under exclusive license to Springer Nature Switzerland AG 2022

This work is subject to copyright. All rights are solely and exclusively licensed by the Publisher, whether the whole or part of the material is concerned, specifically the rights of translation, reprinting, reuse of illustrations, recitation, broadcasting, reproduction on microfilms or in any other physical way, and transmission or information storage and retrieval, electronic adaptation, computer software, or by similar or dissimilar methodology now known or hereafter developed.

The use of general descriptive names, registered names, trademarks, service marks, etc. in this publication does not imply, even in the absence of a specific statement, that such names are exempt from the relevant protective laws and regulations and therefore free for general use.

The publisher, the authors and the editors are safe to assume that the advice and information in this book are believed to be true and accurate at the date of publication. Neither the publisher nor the authors or the editors give a warranty, expressed or implied, with respect to the material contained herein or for any errors or omissions that may have been made. The publisher remains neutral with regard to jurisdictional claims in published maps and institutional affiliations.

This Springer imprint is published by the registered company Springer Nature Switzerland AG
The registered company address is: Gewerbestrasse 11, 6330 Cham, Switzerland

Adrian Wallwork

Giving an Academic Presentation in English

Intermediate Level

Adrian Wallwork
English for Academics
Pisa, Italy

ISSN 2625-3445 ISSN 2625-3453 (electronic)
English for Academic Research
ISBN 978-3-030-95608-0 ISBN 978-3-030-95609-7 (eBook)
https://doi.org/10.1007/978-3-030-95609-7

© The Editor(s) (if applicable) and The Author(s), under exclusive license to Springer Nature Switzerland AG 2022
This work is subject to copyright. All rights are solely and exclusively licensed by the Publisher, whether the whole or part of the material is concerned, specifically the rights of translation, reprinting, reuse of illustrations, recitation, broadcasting, reproduction on microfilms or in any other physical way, and transmission or information storage and retrieval, electronic adaptation, computer software, or by similar or dissimilar methodology now known or hereafter developed.
The use of general descriptive names, registered names, trademarks, service marks, etc. in this publication does not imply, even in the absence of a specific statement, that such names are exempt from the relevant protective laws and regulations and therefore free for general use.
The publisher, the authors and the editors are safe to assume that the advice and information in this book are believed to be true and accurate at the date of publication. Neither the publisher nor the authors or the editors give a warranty, expressed or implied, with respect to the material contained herein or for any errors or omissions that may have been made. The publisher remains neutral with regard to jurisdictional claims in published maps and institutional affiliations.

This Springer imprint is published by the registered company Springer Nature Switzerland AG
The registered company address is: Gewerbestrasse 11, 6330 Cham, Switzerland

Introduction

WHO FOR

- Intermediate to upper intermediate students of academic English
- EAP teachers

TYPE

Self-study guide for students, as well as the basis for a course on academic English.

STRUCTURE OF BOOK

Each chapter covers a specific area of giving presentations, from preparing a script and slides, to giving the presentation (online or at a traditional conference).

STRUCTURE OF CHAPTERS

Each chapter is made up of a series of sections. Most sections begin with a series of questions to get students thinking about the big picture of a specific area of presenting or communicating in general. Then there are explanations and key tips, as well as a series of short exercises.

Contents

1 **The key aims of a presentation** 1
  1.1 What skills do I need to be an academic?
      How do these relate to presentation skills? 1
  1.2 How important are presentation skills? 3
  1.3 What do you dislike about other people's presentations? 4
  1.4 What makes a good presentation? 5
  1.5 What are your fears of giving presentations (in English)? 6
  1.6 How important are first impressions? 8
  1.7 What makes a presentation memorable? 10
  1.8 How different from a scientific/technical
      presentation is a presentation given
      by a humanities/arts student? 12

2 **Resources: Presentations on TED and YouTube** 15
  2.1 What can I learn from watching others give presentations? 15
  2.2 Should I use transcripts and subtitles? 16
  2.3 What presentations should I watch? 19
  2.4 What criteria should I use to assess
      the presentations that I watch? 20
  2.5 Why do I need to speak slowly and clearly? 21
  2.6 Where can I find tips on how to give a good presentation? 24
  2.7 Analysis of two excellent PhD presentations
      available on YouTube 25

3 **Preparing a script before you create the slides** 29
  3.1 Why have a script? 29
  3.2 Do I really need to have a script of the entire presentation? .. 32
  3.3 What are the consequences of not having a script? 33
  3.4 How can I use TED to help me write a script? 36
  3.5 How can I make sure my script is perfect
      from an English point of view? 39

	3.6	How can I use my script to help me with my pronunciation, intonation and tone?	42
	3.7	How should I format/print my script?	44
	3.8	Using Google Translate to translate your script.	47
4	**Pronunciation, intonation, and speed of voice**		49
	4.1	Why do I need to improve my pronunciation?	49
	4.2	How many words will I have to learn how to pronounce correctly?	51
	4.3	Will my accent interfere with the audience's understanding of my English? What other factors might prevent the audience from understanding me?	52
	4.4	How can I check my pronunciation without the help of a teacher?	53
	4.5	Subtitling. How can I check how well a native audience will understand my pronunciation?	56
	4.6	When speaking, what kinds of words do I need to pay special attention to?	59
	4.7	I am very worried that my audience will not understand my English pronunciation. Which sounds do I not need to worry about?	60
5	**Titles**		63
	5.1	What is the purpose of the title slide of a presentation?	63
	5.2	How important are key words in my title?	64
	5.3	I like very simple title slides with no images – to me they seem more professional. Is this a good approach?	66
	5.4	I am a researcher in the Humanities / Arts. How can I make my title more specific?	68
	5.5	Does my title have to be the first slide? Can I put my title in the second or third slide?	69
	5.6	What is essential to include in my title slide? And what can I leave out to create a cleaner slide?	71
6	**Starting your presentation: giving the big picture**		75
	6.1	What is the most important thing I need to know about how to start my presentation?	75
	6.2	How do researchers typically start their presentation? Is this the best way?	77
	6.3	What are some good ways to start a presentation?	79
	6.4	What kinds of questions can I ask my audience at the beginning of my presentation?	80
	6.5	How should I talk about statistics as a way to introduce my research?	82
	6.6	How can I begin by relating my research to my country?	84

	6.7	My research area is very complex. How can I begin in a way that is not too academic and formal?	87
	6.8	My presentation is not for a conference. How should I introduce myself?	89
	6.9	What doesn't the audience need / want to hear in my first 30 seconds?	92
	6.10	How important is my English at the beginning of my presentation?	97
7	**Agenda**		99
	7.1	Do I need an agenda?	99
	7.2	What should I call my agenda? What heading should I use?	101
	7.3	How should I present and explain my agenda?	102
	7.4	When explaining my agenda, should I also mention what I will NOT be covering?	105
	7.5	Is it a good idea to start by giving the audience the 'big picture'?	107
	7.6	When explaining my agenda, how can I encourage the audience to listen carefully and possibly to collaborate with me in the future?	108
	7.7	What tenses in English do I need when outlining my agenda to the audience?	110
8	**Explaining technical slides**		113
	8.1	Why do I need to keep my slides simple?	113
	8.2	I need my audience to see a lot of detail. What can I do?	115
	8.3	Graphs. How should I explain them?	120
	8.4	Bullet points: How do I show them?	123
	8.5	Bullet points to show statistics. How can I use them effectively?	126
	8.6	Statistics. What kind of statistics do audiences like?	128
	8.7	Statistics. How should I present them on my slides?	131
	8.8	Statistics. Can I put different sets of statistics on the same slide?	134
	8.9	Misleading or unclear statistics. What do I need to be aware of?	136
9	**The visual aspect of slides**		139
	9.1	Slide sorter. How can I get an overall view of my presentation?	139
	9.2	Text. How can I limit the amount the number of words in a slide?	142
	9.3	Headers/Slide titles. How big should they be?	145
	9.4	Design Ideas: Are they useful?	147
	9.5	Building a sequence of slides. I want to repeat an element from one slide in the next slide. How should I do this?	153

	9.6	What kind of slides are overused and thus have little effect? Cartoons?	155
	9.7	Should I use fun images?	158
	9.8	Restrictions on the number of slides that can be used. What to do?	160
10	**The conclusions and final slide**		163
	10.1	How should I present my conclusions?	163
	10.2	How can I connect my Conclusions slide with my Final slide?	166
	10.3	What is the real purpose of the final/last slide of my presentation?	169
	10.4	Why should I want the audience to contact me? How do I do so?	171
	10.5	How can I use the limitations of my research to possibly set up a collaboration?	173
	10.6	How can I improve my final slide?	175
	10.7	How important is the final/last slide of a presentation?	179
11	**Q&A Session**		181
	11.1	I am nervous about the Q&A session. How can I prepare for it?	181
	11.2	How should I answer questions at an online conference?	183
	11.3	How should I answer questions at traditional offline conferences?	184
	11.4	What non-technical questions might the audience ask?	186
	11.5	What if I don't understand a question?	187
12	**Doing presentations online**		189
	12.1	What are the pros and cons of doing presentations online?	189
	12.2	How important is my appearance?	192
	12.3	What about my voice? And body language?	194
	12.4	How can I gain and keep audience attention online?	195
	12.5	How can I have minimal text / diagrams in my slides, but also enable my audience to access a very detailed version of my presentation?	197
	12.6	Should my slides be different just because I am online?	198
	12.7	Where can I find tips for using Zoom to help me improve my online presentations?	200
	12.8	What if I have problems connecting and my audience can only hear me but not see my presentation?	202
	12.9	What are the typical mistakes of online presentations?	203

13	**Practising, improving, and getting feedback**		205
	13.1	How should I revise my slides?	205
	13.2	What should I focus on while practising / rehearsing my presentation?	207
	13.3	What should I focus on in the days before an online presentation?	210
	13.4	How can I improve my presentation skills?	213
	13.5	How easy is it to judge one's own performance?	216
	13.6	How should I ask for feedback while preparing my presentation?	217
	13.7	What will I learn if I make a video of me doing my presentation?	219
	13.8	How can I get feedback automatically when rehearsing?	220

Aims of this book.. 223

Other books in this series... 225

Icons 227

FOR EAP TEACHERS: RATIONALE BEHIND THE BOOK AND HOW TO USE IT 229

About the Author... 233

Acknowledgements 235

Index 237

Chapter 1
The key aims of a presentation

1.1 What skills do I need to be an academic? How do these relate to presentation skills?

1. What skills do you need to be an academic today?
2. Are these skills different from those of 20-30 years ago? If so, how?
3. What skills do you already have? Which ones do you think you still need to learn? Why?

Some academics tend to be highly competitive, non-collaborative (i.e. not very interested in sharing results), and focused on publishing or presenting as many papers as possible (i.e. bibliometric indicators). Other aspects of academic life, such as teaching and solving the problems of society, are given low priority as they are considered as being unproductive because they don't further an academic's career.

However, there is also a trend towards more open science and more open data infrastructures. Thus it is now considered important to conduct research that

- enables others to collaborate and contribute
- encourages the free availability of data, procedures, protocols etc, so that results can be replicated, re-used and redistributed
- has a clear goal, i.e. is mission-oriented
- will benefit society in general, i.e. will not just be of interest to a small group of researchers

1.1 What skills do I need to be an academic? How do these relate to presentation skills? (cont.)

This means that you will need to learn more about how to communicate your results clearly and to collaborate with others. Such communication skills involve:

- being open-minded and flexible, with an ability to debate constructively
- developing relationships with your local community and with the community of scientists
- coordinating projects

Obviously, you still need to show excellence and rigor in your research. But no matter how good your results are, if you cannot communicate them well (orally or written), they will have little real value. If you want a successful and rewarding career you need to learn to present well – and this book will teach you how!

Audiences at conferences need to see the VALUE of your work easily and quickly.

Being an academic, you probably don't spend much time thinking about market and commercial forces. However, your job at a presentation is to inform and possibly 'persuade' your audience. If they 'buy' these ideas, i.e. if they can see the clear value of what you are saying, then you are more likely to have a successful career.

One of the PhD students who attended my class on scientific communication in English was studying dark matter, i.e. material that we can't see but seems likely to exist in space. Her research involves highly complex mathematical calculations. Her presentations were very dry and she seemed to be talking to a very small audience of other physicists like herself. The result was that other students in her course showed minimal interest in what she was saying. However, after the course she emailed me the message below. I have highlighted the most relevant points in italics.

> *After your suggestions, I recorded myself many times on Zoom to practice saying my script in a more enthusiastic way.* I also showed the YouTube recording of my presentation to friends and colleagues for *more feedback*. I'll continue to think of making *my topic more relatable to any audience*, it's a very useful idea. It has also *helped me to think of what I am doing as more than just a calculation*.

She had thus understood the importance of showing her passion for her research, of sharing her work (including her presentations) with colleagues in order to hear their opinions, and to see her research as having a wider scope than just dealing with very large numbers.

1.2 How important are presentation skills?

- Why is it important to give presentations at international conferences?
- Executives in industry often consider communication skills to be more relevant than technical skills. Why do you think this is? Do you think that also university professors consider communication skills to be so important? Why (not)?

Below is a list of the benefits of giving a presentation. Which three are the most important for you personally?

1. Exploit the review process that takes place before the conference. (When you submit an abstract of a presentation for a conference, you will generally receive feedback from the conference reviewers).
2. Travel to interesting places (when no virus restrictions are in place!).
3. Gain visibility– helps you to increase your chances of establishing new contacts, collaborating with other research groups, and getting more funds.
4. Network and meet up with old friends, colleagues and people who - until now - you may have only contacted via email or Zoom.
5. Get new ideas while listening and talking to other people, and find out what the hot topics are and what other researchers are working on.
6. Encourage the audience to read your paper on the same topic.
7. Talk about things that you probably wouldn't mention in your paper, e.g. ideas and hypotheses, negative results, unfinished work - all of these might stimulate useful questions and feedback from the audience.
8. Include a reference to a presentation you have made in your CV and in applications for grants.
9. Prepare yourself for a career in industry - in the future, if you work for a company you will certainly have to give presentations for products and services, proposals, and progress reports.

If you give a good informative and entertaining presentation people will:

1. be interested in what you do and want to learn more
2. may be interested in collaborating with you
3. may invite you to their university
4. may give you funds to continue your research

1.3 What do you dislike about other people's presentations?

Make a list of five things about other people's presentations that you don't like.

Compare your answers with the key. Which factors listed in the key were not things that you thought of? How important are they?

1. Lack of preparation and practice
2. No eye contact with audience
3. No clear structure / No clear message
4. Too much text – hard to find key info
5. No images
6. Presenter reads the text / Monotone voice
7. Too long + too many technical details
8. Too many animations
9. Too small fonts, bad use of color
10. No match between speech and slides
11. No real conclusion or call for action
12. ONLINE: slow at uploading presentation, eyes down, big headphones, background noise, strange virtual background, obviously reading speech

1.4 What makes a good presentation?

Below are eight key skills needed to make a good presentation.

Which skills do you:

   a) already have?

   b) want to learn?

   c) think are not particularly relevant?

1. Captivating introduction: immediately connects with the audience
2. Clear description of problem + goal + results
3. Clear slides: essential info that audience can understand and absorb quickly
4. Clear message: nothing difficult to understand - audience feels positive
5. Delivery and tone: passionate, convincing, interesting, enthusiastic, and confident
6. Speech: normal voice (not in 'presentation mode'), not fast, with frequent pauses
7. Authentic: transparent about limitations; not worried about seeming vulnerable
8. Memorable: audience remembers you as a person (not just what you said), so that they will be encouraged to contact you, keep in touch, and possibly collaborate

In order to demonstrate the skills listed above and deliver a good presentation, it is ESSENTIAL that you really understand:

- why you chose your specific research – what problem you are trying to solve and why
- why this research is important to you and why you find it interesting
- why it is important to tell other people about your research
- what would happen if NO ONE did your research

✐

Write answers to at least two of the points above. Think very carefully before you start writing.

1.5 What are your fears of giving presentations (in English)?

One in four Americans are afraid of speaking in public. Are you? Why?

Which three of the eight 'fears' listed below are you most afraid of?

1. Being center of attention
2. Being judged – feeling stupid compared to profs in audience
3. Losing track
4. Not feeling prepared
5. Not being clear or understood
6. Getting + keeping audience attention
7. English (pronunciation + grammar)
8. Q & A session

What can you do to overcome the eight fears listed above?

See the key for some practical solutions.

The key factor is to enjoy yourself. If you enjoy yourself you will automatically give an engaging presentation. To enjoy yourself you need to know why you find your research interesting and why it is important to tell others about it. If you don't know why, you will NEVER give a good presentation.

If you are new to presenting, try practicing in low-risk situations, for example internal presentations in front of colleagues.

If you do not like being the center of attention, then try to overcome this fear by gradually building up your confidence by:

- offering to teach undergraduates – this is a great way to learn presentation skills and to become at ease at talking to a big group of people
- participating more actively in meetings, e.g. voicing your opinion rather than remaining silent
- taking part in activities outside work such as team sports, acting clubs, speakers' clubs
- beginning conversations with strangers on buses, trains and planes

1.5 What are your fears of giving presentations (in English)? (cont.)

Solutions to fears

1. Practice being the center of attention in your everyday life. With family, friends, colleagues try not to be the one who stays silent. Instead, talk more. Prepare in advance things that you can say to people. Take up hobbies that put you at the center of attention: acting, dancing, playing music etc

2. Your professors were once PhD students. They know how you are feeling. With a few exceptions, the audience is always on your side, they want you to do well, they are not judging you. Sometimes there are professors and senior researchers in the audience. They may be looking for new people to join their research team. They may want to see how well you express yourself and communicate, even if your presentation is not brilliant.

3. When you are NOT doing an online presentation, you can hold written notes in your hand or upload your presentation onto your phone so that you can look at it while giving your presentation.

4. You have no excuse for not feeling prepared or not being clear. You must practice practice practice practice practice practice practice practice.

5. Same as 4.

6. Use a personal story, an interesting counterintuitive statistic, a question, a video. Do NOT simply introduce yourself and your topic.

7. Use Google Translate (or other applications) for the pronunciation – see 4.4. Have a few individual lessons with an English teacher to practice your speech and giving the presentation.

8. Get family and friends and colleagues to ask you as many questions as possible. Note down the questions and, if possible, have the answers integrated into your slides. In any case prepare answers for all the questions. This will also increase the chances of you hearing the question during the Q&A. Arrange with a colleague or friendly person that you have met at the conference to ask you the first question. If you don't understand a question, admit it. Say "I'm sorry, I am not sure if I have understood the question. Could you ask me again during the coffee break"? See Chapter 11.

1.6 How important are first impressions?

1. How fast do you think professional recruiters judge a CV?
2. How quickly do you think you form an impression of another person?
3. How important is the impression you give in the first seconds of your presentation?

1) 6 seconds!
2) 4-10 seconds.
3) Very. If you make a good first impression the audience are more likely to i) watch your presentation with attention; ii) forgive you if you make mistakes or if they don't always understand exactly what you are saying.

A good first impression tends to be a lasting impression. This means that you will have to do a lot of negative things to make the person re-evaluate their initial positive impression.

This doesn't mean that if you are very nervous at the beginning of your presentation and make, for example, mistakes with your English, that the audience will have a terrible impression and stop listening to you. It simply means that you will have to compensate by having good clear slides, by giving interesting and pertinent information etc.

1.6 How important are first impressions? (cont.)

To learn more about how quickly you form an impression of someone, watch 30-60 seconds of the four conference presentations below. They are just a random selection.

        https://www.youtube.com/watch?v=ovH2LLuR_Zc

        https://www.youtube.com/watch?v=F7jehSHLpK8

        https://www.youtube.com/watch?v=k588C2dMLCY

        https://www.youtube.com/watch?v=8WB0OIM5RlE

Don't worry about the topic or whether you understand what they are saying. Just think about your impression of the presenter. The questions below are designed to help you formulate your impression.

1. Do they look competent and professional?
2. If you knew all the terminology, do you think you would be able to follow what they are saying?
3. Would you like to meet them?
4. Which presenter gave you the best impression? Why?
5. What have you learned from this exercise? How could you improve the first impression that others have of you?

1.7 What makes a presentation memorable?

Why do you remember some presentations and instantly forget others?

Below are links to four presentations (but you can search for others if you want):

> https://www.youtube.com/watch?v=HrnTZND1a_0&t=97s
>
> https://www.youtube.com/watch?v=RfoF2SCboJ0
>
> https://www.youtube.com/watch?v=7FfKaIgArJ8&t=20s
>
> https://www.youtube.com/watch?v=XrflFPDbD98

Watch two or three minutes of each presentation, or more if you find the presentation interesting.

Wait for a day to pass before answering the four questions below.

1. Which presentation do you remember the most in terms of the impression it had on you?
2. Write down three things that you remember about each presentation in terms of statistics, information and general content.
3. Watch the presentations again. How much of the information had you forgotten?
4. What have you learned from this experience?

When we think about the presentations we have seen, what we often remember is the presenter rather than what he/she presented.

We remember whether

- we liked the presenter as a person – they were friendly, approachable, not too slick (i.e. not perfect)
- we understood what they were saying, i.e. they didn't speak too quickly and the concepts were not too difficult to grasp
- we found their delivery/technique effective e.g. they managed to attract and keep our attention through telling their story, through an interesting or counter-intuitive statistic, by asking us a question that we could personally relate to
- they explained things easily without taxing our brains
- we continued to think about the presentation after the presentation had finished

1.7 What makes a presentation memorable? (cont.)

Often what we remember is <u>not</u> WHAT information the presenter gave us, but more HOW we were given the information and whether we liked the person WHO gave us the information.

Consequently, the main aim of your presentation is not merely to give information, but above all to be MEMORABLE.

If your presentation is memorable, people will want to meet you (during the coffee break, at the social dinner, at future conferences), contact you, read your paper, and collaborate with you.

If they collaborate with you, then you will increase your chances of getting funds for your research.

The main aim of a presentation is that you and your presentation are memorable. You make the audience interested in you and your work to the extent that they want to collaborate in some way.

1.8 How different from a scientific/technical presentation is a presentation given by a humanities/arts student?

This subsection is for those readers/students are who are studying for example, literature, history, political/social sciences, or anthropology.

Read the difference between the natural sciences and humanities in this definition from Wikipedia:

> The natural sciences seek to derive general laws through reproducible and verifiable experiments. The humanities generally study local traditions, through their history, literature, music, and arts, with an emphasis on understanding particular individuals, events, or eras. (Source: https://en.wikipedia.org/wiki/Humanities)

Does this difference mean that not all the guidelines mentioned so far in this section (and the rest of this book) do not necessarily apply to presentations given by humanities students?

For example, is it acceptable for humanities students:

1. to give presentations that are predominantly text-based and contain few images?

2. not to justify why they do their research and therefore avoid any practical relevance of their research to current world problems?

1.8 How different from a scientific/technical presentation is a presentation given by a humanities/arts student? (cont.)

During my courses on scientific English, I have heard the following comments from humanities students who were initially reluctant to follow the strategies I outline in this book. I personally do not agree with them.

- You do not have to justify why you are doing your particular research or why it is important.
- If your topic is, for example, medieval history, there is absolutely no need to relate to an analogous problem in current times.
- It is important to sound intelligent and use complex phrases.
- Images are an optional, and are probably not suitable for humanities presentations.
- You should have a serious look on your face at all times.
- You do not need to try and make a real connection with the audience.

I believe that most (if not all) the guidelines given in this book are applicable not only to science students, but also to all humanities students. Your aim is to share your research with as many people as possible, and not necessarily exclusively to people in your field. Clearly, if you are a humanities student and do not agree with a particular guideline then you can ignore it (although I do ask you to at least consider it).

Chapter 2
Resources: Presentations on TED and YouTube

2.1 What can I learn from watching others give presentations?

1. Have you ever taken part in an online conference (either just watching or also giving a presentation)? What were your impressions? How effective and memorable were the presentations?
2. Have you seen any TED presentations? Do you have any favorites?
3. What can you learn from online presentations that will help you improve your presentation skills?

Learning how to do presentations can take several years and there is always something new to learn. Part of this process is watching other people do their presentations. You can note down the things that they do well (which you can imitate), and the things that you find are ineffective and can thus avoid in your own presentations.

2.2 Should I use transcripts and subtitles?

If you have never been on the ted.com website, now is the time! Familiarize yourself with all the features:

You can:

- search for a particular topic using TED's search engine
- show English subtitles (and often subtitles in your own language)
- see or download a full transcript (called 'interactive transcript') of the presentation in English, plus translations in several other languages.
- note down any useful phrases that the speaker uses that you think you could use too
- improve your pronunciation and intonation by trying to imitate the presenter

When watching videos in English (not just presentations, but also shows, series and movies on Netflix, TV, YouTube etc):

1. Do you watch with subtitles in English? Why (not)?
2. Do you ever watch with subtitles in your own language? Why (not)?
3. If transcripts of the video are available, how do you use them?

1. The subtitles on TED report every single word. However, for movies and TV series, the subtitles may be an abbreviated version of what has been said. In terms of presentations, subtitles (and transcripts) are very useful for seeing (not just hearing) how many words a presenter uses in a sentence. This highlights that the shorter the sentence is, the easier it is for the presenter to say, and the easier it is for the audience to understand.

2. There are no rules for whether you should watch with or without subtitles. My suggestion is that you vary what you do. So sometimes without subtitles, sometimes in English, sometimes in your own language (particularly for parts that are difficult to understand, or simply to give yourself a break).

2.2 Should I use transcripts and subtitles? (cont.)

3. A key benefit of a transcript is that you can read it before you watch, either in English or, on TED, in your own language if this is available. This means that you won't have to concentrate as much on listening or reading the subtitles while you are actually watching the presentation. On TED you can stop and start the transcript wherever you like. If you like a particular presenter's way of speaking, you can practice reading aloud from the script and see if you can imitate the presenter's intonation and general pronunciation.

When watching presentations on YouTube, you can activate:

1) Subtitles (see the pink circle in the menu at the bottom on the right of the screenshot below).

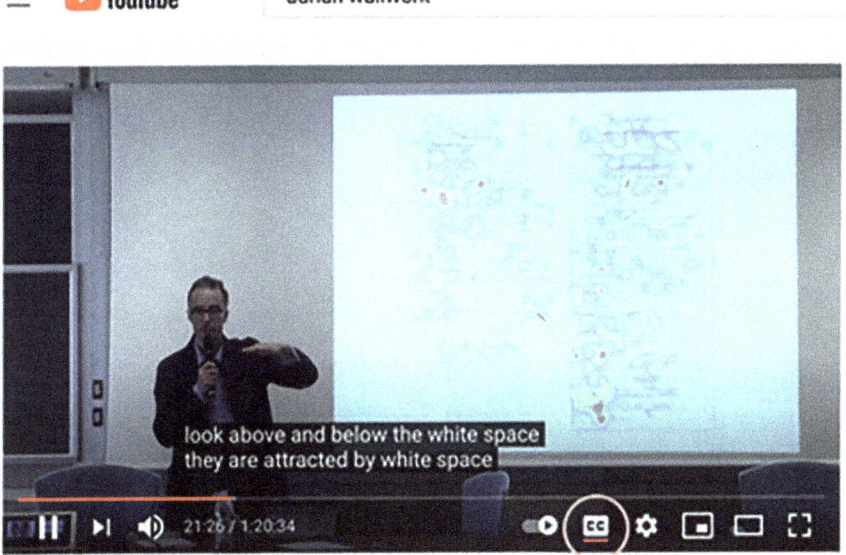

Lezione 7 (pt1) - Adrian Wallwork, "How to write a CV and a cover letter"

2.2 Should I use transcripts and subtitles? (cont.)

2) A transcript of what you are watching. From settings (...) 'Open transcript'.

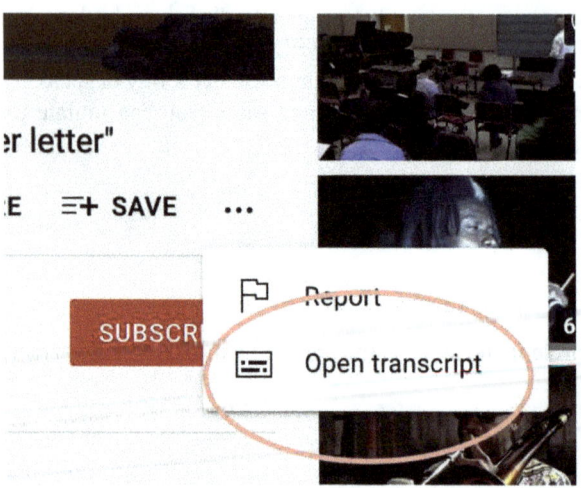

You will then see the automatically generated transcript on the right.

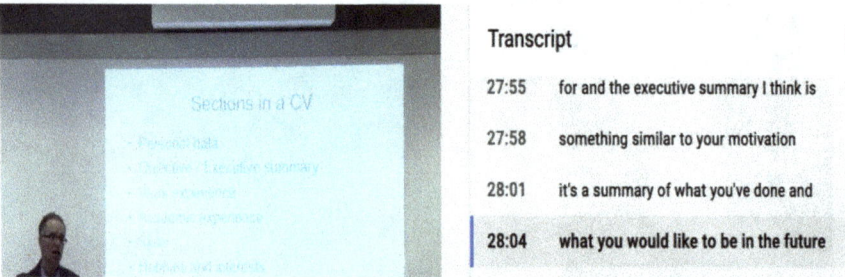

You can even find transcripts for your favorite movie. Use a Google search: "movie transcripts". The site below is reasonably reliable:

https://transcripts.fandom.com/wiki/List_of_Movies

2.3 What presentations should I watch?

There is a massive choice of presentations available online:

- academic presentations given by professors / PhD students, and people from the worlds of art, sports, business, politics etc.
- old (starting at the beginning of this millennium) and new
- with slides and without

To help you specifically with presentations, I suggest you watch presentations:

- on ted.com
- three-minute thesis presentations given by PhD students. Many universities hold competitions for the best 3-minute presentation given by PhD students. You can find these on YouTube by searching for "Three minute thesis" or "Three minute presentation" or "3MT winner".
- of entire congresses / conferences – just watch 30 seconds of 5-10 presentations, and decide which ones are the most effective and why
- on how to present – there are a lot of experts giving their advice on YouTube. Search for "conference presentations" or "how to speak at conference" or "how to give a great research talk" etc.
- on how to present specific parts of your presentation: "how to open and close presentations", "how to start a presentation" etc.
- on how NOT to present: "bad presentations".

The style of presentations delivered on TED has had a huge impact on how presenters in academia (business etc) now give presentations.

Until around 2015 most presentations on TED contained slides and the presenters were not necessarily as well prepared as they are today – now everything is scripted and rehearsed many many times, and there is a lot of focus on the presenter's charisma. So you can probably learn more from the older presentations on TED than from the new ones. And this is probably also true for the student presentations that win prizes – today they are heavily influenced by the TED formula of giving presentations, and this TED formula may not be appropriate for the academic conference where you are presenting.

2.4 What criteria should I use to assess the presentations that I watch?

When watching a presentation online, don't just sit and watch passively. Think critically about what makes it a good or bad presentation – in this way you will learn how to improve your own presentation techniques. To help you assess the presentations that you watch, the table below gives you suggestions on what to look for.

	PRESENTER TENDS TO DO THIS (GOOD)	RATHER THAN THIS (BAD)
CORE FOCUS	clarifies main point of presentation immediately - it is clear to audience why they should listen	main point only emerges towards end - not clear where presentation is going
STRUCTURE	each new point is organically connected to the previous point	there are no clear transitions or connections
PACE / SPEED	varies pace: speaks slowly for key points, faster for more obvious information; pauses occasionally	maintains the same speed throughout; no pauses
DELIVERY	sounds natural, enthusiastic, sincere	sounds rather robotic and non-spontaneous
BODY LANGUAGE	eyes on audience, moves hands, stands away from the screen, moves around	eyes on screen, PC, ceiling, floor; static, blocks screen
STYLE	narrative: you want to hear what happened next; lots of personal pronouns and active forms of verbs	technical, passive forms
LANGUAGE	dynamic, adjectives, very few linkers (*also, in addition, moreover, in particular*)	very formal, no emotive adjectives, many linkers
AUDIENCE INVOLVEMENT	involves / entertains the audience - thus maintaining their attention	seems to be talking to him/herself
TEXT IN SLIDES	little or no text	too much text
GRAPHICS	simple graphics or complex graphics built up gradually	complex graphics
ABSTRACT VS CONCRETE	gives examples	focuses on abstract theory
STATISTICS	gives counterintuitive / interesting facts	makes little or no use of facts / statistics
AT THE END	you feel inspired / positive	you are indifferent

2.5 Why do I need to speak slowly and clearly?

One TED talk, from 2009, is a 4-minute presentation called 'English Mania'. The presenter, Jay Walker, talks about the importance of learning English.

He talks very slowly, using very short sentences. Here is how he begins:

> Let's talk about manias. Let's start with Beatle mania: hysterical teenagers, crying, screaming, pandemonium. Sports mania: deafening crowds, all for one idea -- get the ball in the net. Okay, religious mania: there's rapture, there's weeping, there's visions. Manias can be good. Manias can be alarming. Or manias can be deadly.
>
> The world has a new mania. A mania for learning English. Listen as Chinese students practice their English by screaming it.

In the 60-second extract above, he uses: 72 words divided into 10 sentences. That's an average of 7.2 words per sentence - much less than 100 words per minute.

Watch 'English Mania'.

http://www.ted.com/talks/jay_walker_on_the_world_s_english_mania?language=en

Before watching read the following questions:

1. Who do you think his audience is?
2. How does he structure his presentation? What is the purpose of the structure? Do you like it?
3. How does he modulate his voice (i.e. so that it is not just a monotone)?
4. What type of words does he stress in particular?
5. Does he use traditional slides?
6. What does he use in case he forgets what he is going to say?
7. Does he smile?
8. Could you do this kind of presentation at a conference? Why? Why not?
9. What aspects of his presentation and delivery could you usefully imitate/adopt?

After you have watched once, think about your answers to the questions above, and then watch again. Finally, discuss the questions.

2.5 Why do I need to speak slowly and clearly? (cont.)

1) SHORT SENTENCES AND SIMPLE LANGUAGE. Jay is talking to an audience of primarily native English speakers. So why does he adopt this style? Well, he knows that if you want your audience to understand your message quickly and easily (i.e. with no mental effort on their part) then you need to have a clear structure and to speak in the simplest way possible (but not as if you are talking to a child).

Also, by using short sentences, it helps him to:

- remember what he wants to say
- speak clearly without hesitation

Jay's style of speaking is exactly the same as the NASA engineer's style of writing which you can find in the companion book English for Writing Research Papers (3.17), where again the writer is writing for an audience of native English speakers and uses very short sentences and simple vocabulary.

2) STRUCTURE Jay does not immediately talk about his main topic, i.e. English. Instead, he introduces the theme, i.e. manias. This gives the audience (particularly any non-natives) time to tune into his voice. So consider having a 30 second introduction to your presentation where the audience hear something interesting and relevant, but not crucial. It will also help you to settle your nerves.

3, 4) VOICE AND INTONATION. Overall, Jay speaks slowly. However, like all good presenters he tends to say less important information (non-key words) quickly, but then pauses on the key words and says them louder. He often slows down to focus on numbers/statistics and on emotive adjectives. This provides variety in his voice/tone and also helps the audience to understand when he is saying something important or interesting.

5) SLIDES Jay does not use any written slides, only images. This may work if your message is incredibly clear and requires little or no mental effort on the part of the audience. He uses his slides to remind him what to say and to help the audience follow what he is saying. However, international audiences generally appreciate slides with at least some text on them. This means that if they can't understand what you are saying, they can at least follow your slides.

6) NOTES He has notes in his hand. He recognizes his own limitations. He may forget what he is saying. He is confident enough to know that it is perfectly acceptable to take a quick look at these notes even at a very important conference.

2.5 Why do I need to speak slowly and clearly? (cont.)

7) SMILING Even though he doesn't smile a lot, he compensates by being interesting - he packs his presentations with weird and wonderful statistics (but always pertinent).

8, 9) IS JAY'S STYLE SUITABLE FOR A CONFERENCE Probably not. It is not an academic presentation. However, my main reason for suggesting that you watch this presentation is to understand that speaking slowly and clearly is key to giving a good presentation, along with an introduction where you give your audience time to tune in to your voice and topic.

Don't worry if you are not a natural presenter, or you are a little stiff (rigid) in your body language, or you have to look at your notes, or you make a couple of mistakes with your English. What is most important is that you give a clear message in a way that is effortless for the audience to understand.

Parts of the section were originally in 19.5 of *English for Presentations at International Conferences.*

2.6 Where can I find tips on how to give a good presentation?

Below are links to four YouTube videos on how to give a good presentation: some refer to conferences, others to three-minute presentations given by PhD students (see 2.7).

        https://www.youtube.com/watch?v=z5hgbVDPZsQ

        https://www.youtube.com/watch?v=U9czKztZK1I&t=175s

        https://www.youtube.com/watch?v=vZFxJ_PGWOc

        https://www.youtube.com/watch?v=S5c1susCPAE

For each person note down the tips they give and then discuss the following questions.

1. Which two presenters did you understand the best? Why?

2. Which presenter did you like the most why? Why?

3. Which was the worst presenter? Why?

4. Taking into account all four videos, which three tips were the most useful for you?

There are hundreds of videos on YouTube teaching you how to give a good presentation. Some focus on the first 2-3 slides, others on the entire presentation. To find such videos type in "tips for * presentations", "tips for conference presentations", "how to present at conferences" etc.

2.7 Analysis of two excellent PhD presentations available on YouTube

Imagine your professor tells you to take part in a competition where you have only three minutes to present your research in front of a live audience (not online).

1. How difficult would it be for you to reduce your normal presentations to three minutes?
2. Would it be a good idea to speak faster than normal so that you could cover as much information as possible?
3. What would you cut from your normal presentation?
4. Would you use slides or just talk without slides?
5. How would you dress?
6. How would you attract the audience's attention at the beginning?
7. How would you end your presentation?
8. Would you try to smile?
9. How much would you use your hands and move around?
10. How nervous would you be? What could you do to reduce/control your nerves?

Now watch these two presentations. Both presenters won prizes for their presentations, so they are both very good. However, about 80% of my students (irrespectively of gender and nationality) have quite a strong preference for one of the presenters.

As you watch, think about how you answered the ten questions above. When you have finished watching, decide which presenter you prefer. Turn on the transcript feature (see screenshot in 2.2).

https://www.youtube.com/watch?v=7YesMSG9izE

https://www.youtube.com/watch?v=dexCh39jEg4

2.7 Analysis of two excellent PhD presentations available on YouTube (cont.)

Analysis of Willemijn Doedens's presentation

(0.00) No introduction of herself. Gets you to imagine a situation in order to prepare you for the theoretical/technical part.

(0.25) Gives a clear definition: *aphasia is a language impairment, often caused by stroke, which is a disruption of the blood flow to the brain.*

(0.49) Current situation.

(1.07) The problem.

(1.14) Returns to her example to then explain her aim.

(1.37) Aim of research.

(1.46) What is known already as a motivation for doing her research.

(2.34) More about the aim of her research in a non-technical way.

(2.43) Her methodology.

(2.54) Conclusion: How her research will help people.

Five key points about her delivery

1. She speaks slowly and very clearly.
2. She is dressed quite formally.
3. She uses no slides.
4. We only see the top half of her body, but she gives a lot of expression through her face and hands. She doesn't really smile, but she seems passionate about her research.
5. She seems very natural, very unpretentious, and thus very approachable. But at the same time she's very professional.

2.7 Analysis of two excellent PhD presentations available on YouTube (cont.)

Analysis of Frob Duguid's presentation

(0.21 – start of presentation): No introduction of himself. Immediately states purpose of his thesis.

(0.29) Asks audience a question. Gets them actively involved.

(0.41) Current situation (as confirmed by audience's answers)

(0.47) Gives interesting statistic – audiences love statistics particularly if the statistic somehow relates to them personally.

(0.52) The problem.

(1.01) Relates the problem to something the audience experience themselves. Adds another statistic.

(1.14) Having said the bad news, now moves to the good news.

(1.24) Prepares audience for his research aim.

(1.33) Methodology.

(1.55) Results.

(2.08) Repeats key point to ensure the audience heard it.

(2.16) Work that still needs to be done.

(2.25) Another example to help the audience to understand the scope of the problem that he is investigating.

(2.35) Ends with a suggestion for the audience that will help them avoid the kinds of problems he has been discussing.

Five key points about his delivery

1. He speaks in a very animated and passionate way. He is extremely good at capturing the audience's attention. A non-native audience might find him a little too fast.
2. He is dressed very formally. NB: Be careful what you wear, not everyone is a fan of bow ties!
3. He uses some slides.
4. He moves around a lot. His enthusiasm is also revealed by the way he uses his hands and arms continuously. Note: How much you move and what you do with your hands will also depend on your culture.
5. He seems extremely professional.

2.7 Analysis of two excellent PhD presentations available on YouTube (cont.)

Frob's presentation has a perfect structure, there is a lot of variety, and massive audience engagement. It is difficult to find criticisms. He has certainly practised this presentation many many times and certainly deserved to win a prize. He gives his message very effectively.

Willemijn's approach was less engaging, but seemed more natural. Importantly, Willemijn spoke more slowly, she wanted you to understand her easily. This naturalness combined with speaking slowly may be preferred by some audiences to Frob's more animated approach.

If you analyse presentations in the same way as I have above, you can learn a lot about how to:

- structure your presentation
- begin and end
- use examples before theory
- talk about the problem and then your solution
- talk slowly and clearly

English for Presentations at International Conferences. Chapter 2 contains more analysis of TED talks.

Chapter 3
Preparing a script before you create the slides

3.1 Why have a script?

Below is an example of a script for a presentation.

> Good morning. I'm XX and I would like to talk to you about the epigenetic clock. First of all I want to explain to you what epigenetic is.
>
> Epigenetic is a branch of molecular biology, which studies heritable changes in gene function and expression that do not involve alterations in DNA sequences.
>
> We usually use chronological age to measure aging, but it does not always correspond to biological age.

1. Do you use a script? Why? Why not?
2. Does your choice of whether to use a script or not depend on whether you are doing a presentation online or live?
3. Which of the following are good reasons for NOT preparing a script for your presentation?

    a) It is important to be spontaneous and to improvise occasionally.

    b) If I had a script I would just read it and the audience would know that I was reading from my script.

    c) If you rehearse (practise) a lot then you don't need a script.

    d) It is not professional.

Now check with the key.

NONE of the four reasons are good reasons for not having a script. As you will see in this chapter, preparing a script is ESSENTIAL to giving a good presentation.

3.1 Why have a script? (cont.)

a) It is certainly not a negative thing to appear spontaneous. However, if you are spontaneous and improvise you will very probably:

- make more mistakes with your English because you are saying words and phrases that you have not practised during your preparation
- lose track of what you are saying
- take more time than you had planned and thus risk going over your allotted time slot

b) Nobody likes seeing a presenter reading a script. However, if you are doing your presentation online, you can have it on your screen without the audience seeing it. The important thing is to not to focus your eyes always on the script, but to move your eyes and head slightly as you would when looking at a live audience.

c) Even some professional presenters forget what they want to say in the middle of giving their presentation. Yes, practising is essential. But on the big day it is normal to feel nervous. Having a script to refer to will give you added confidence. You are not forced to use your script, but at least you know it is there if you need it.

d) The presenters that you see on ted.com (see Chapter 2) all begin their preparation by writing a script. This is why there is very little redundancy in what they say, and they use short clear sentences. Clearly, they don't actually read their script while presenting, but they do use a script in the preparation phase.

Discuss the reasons given in the key to the previous exercise on the reasons why you should write a script.

Do you now think it is a good idea to prepare a script? If you are still not convinced, read the reasons given below.

3.1 Why have a script? (cont.)

Writing a script has many advantages both when you are preparing your slides and when you are delivering your presentation live.

PREPARATION PHASE

1. use it as a basis for preparing your slides – typically people prepare their slides first and then decide what they are going to say, however the reverse procedure is generally more effective

2. decide exactly how you are going to begin your presentation. To learn more about this see Chapter 6.

3. keep revising it (e.g. reducing the amount you say, keeping only what the audience really needs to know) so that it is structured perfectly, flows well, and allows you to speak slowly and clearly

4. understand what sentences are difficult to say – you can then modify/shorten them

5. understand what words you are unable to pronounce – you can do this by listening to your speech using Google Translate (or another application). To learn more about this see Chapter 4.

WHEN SCRIPT AND SLIDES ARE READY

6. email your speech to an English-speaking colleague to revise or you can even submit it to a professional service. Then you can be sure that at least the grammar and vocabulary will be correct. This will give you confidence and make you feel less nervous

7. show your speech to a colleague (without forcing them to watch you performing)—this is a quick way to see if your presentation is clear and interesting.

8. decide what the best structure is and thus the best order for your slides, and if certain slides can be cut

IN FRONT OF LIVE AUDIENCE

9. refer to it while doing the presentation – so if you lose track or forget what you planned to say next, you can take a quick look at your script (or notes on your script)

Writing a script thus helps you both in the preparation and practise phases AND while you are giving the presentation to your audience. You are not forced to use it during the live presentation, but there are so many good reasons for using it during the preparation phase that I would say a script is ESSENTIAL.

3.2 Do I really need to have a script of the entire presentation?

Imagine you don't have time to write a script for your entire presentation. Which parts of the presentation would benefit the most from having a well-prepared script?

    a) the first 2-3 slides and the last two slides

    b) the technical parts

How many words do you think you would say in a ten-minute presentation?

    a) 1000 b) 1500 c) 3000

I strongly suggest that you write down everything. A typical ten-minute presentation only requires 1200–1800 words.

The beginnings and endings of presentations tend to be less technical. These are the places where presenters tend to improvise the most. When you improvise you tend to hesitate more, make more mistakes and be less time efficient. At least 20% of the words and phrases that inexperienced presenters use tend to be redundant, i.e., they give no information that is useful for the audience. That's 20% less time for explaining and emphasizing the key points. This is why you must have a script for the beginning and ending of your presentation.

However, for the more technical parts of the presentation, when you explain your methodology and results, it may be enough to write notes. This is because these technical aspects will probably be the easiest for you to talk about, as you will be very familiar with them and will probably have all the correct English terminology that you need.

Writing a script is NOT like writing a paper

- Be relatively informal (don't speak like you were reading your paper aloud).
- Make it sound like you are telling a story. You are NOT just telling your readers about your methods and findings like you would in a paper.
- Use personal pronouns (*I, my, we, our*)
- Use much shorter sentences.
- Eliminate all redundancy.

3.3 What are the consequences of not having a script?

Do you know what the term 'technology transfer' means?

Read this definition of 'technology transfer' from the website of the European Commission:

> Technology transfer (TT) refers to the process of conveying results stemming from scientific and technological research to the marketplace and to wider society, along with associated skills and procedures, and is as such an intrinsic part of the technological innovation process.

https://knowledge4policy.ec.europa.eu/technology-transfer/what-technology-transfer_en

Below is a script of the beginning of a presentation on technology transfer. The presentation was given by one of my Italian PhD students, Ilaria. As you read, think about these two questions:

1. How different is her definition from the one given by the European Commission?
2. Is what she says suitable for the beginning of a presentation? Will it attract the audience's attention? Why/Why not?

> Technology transfer works to complement academic research by innovation out of the lab door into the hands of industry partners who will develop them into products for the benefit of the general public. If you believe you have discovered something unique - you have a new idea - it is important to protect it.
>
> For example, the value of any new technology must be demonstrated through a series of increasingly stringent steps and requires a long time.

Ilaria's opening words a typical of many academics: a long series of generic abstract statements. There are no examples or statistics to get the audience focused. What she says sounds like it has been written for a textbook or website, not for a live audience. If a presentation begins like this, most audiences will lose their interest within about 30 seconds.

If you have a script, you can analyse it in every detail. You can keep improving it. It is much more difficult to make such improvements if you don't have the text of your speech to work on.

3.3 What are the consequences of not having a script? (cont.)

At the beginning of a presentation you need to get to the point immediately, eliminate any unsubstantiated claims, and replace abstract terminology with concrete words and examples.

A much better script would be to eliminate the above introduction completely.

In Ilaria's second attempt to write the beginning of her speech, she decided to have a photo of some researcher friends of hers and to use them as an example of how technology transfer works.

> These are some friends of mine. They want to develop a kit for detecting breast cancer in a non-invasive way. They are part of a team of researchers studying genomics. The problem is that their technology could remain unknown if no one funds their research. And this means that around 3000 women per year here in Italy could fail to have their breast cancer diagnosed. Breast cancer is the most common form of cancer among women - 42% of cancer cases. It is the leading cause of cancer death amongst women. Interestingly, breast cancer also affects men - one in a thousand in Italy.

The new version is much more personal. It enables Ilaria to inject some passion into her voice. The audience will understand why she is studying technology transfer and how important it can be. She also manages to get all the audience involved by referring to male breast cancer too.

Note how in Ilaria's revised version the sentences are much shorter. This means they are i) easier for her to remember, and ii) easier for her to say.

By having a script you can understand which sentences are difficult to say.

How easy would it be for you to say the following in a presentation?

> The main advantages of these techniques are a minimum or absent sample pre-treatment and a quick response; in fact due to the relative difficulty in the interpretation of the obtained mass spectra, the use of multivariate analysis by principal component analysis, and complete-linkage cluster analysis of mass spectral data, that is to say the relative abundance of peaks, was used as a tool for rapid comparison, differentiation, and classification of the samples.

Now rewrite it using shorter sentences. If you prefer, you can try to re-write something that YOU have written.

3.3 What are the consequences of not having a script? (cont.)

Below is a possible solution:

> There are two main advantages to these techniques. First, the sample needs very little or no pre-treatment. Second, you get a quick response. Mass spectra are really hard to interpret. So we decided to use two types of analysis: principal component and complete-linkage cluster. We did the analysis on the relative abundance of peaks. All this meant that we could compare, differentiate, and classify the samples.

Try reading the original and the answer given in the key.

You will notice that the original is very difficult to say in one breath (i.e. without stopping to inhale). If it is difficult for you to say, you can imagine that it will be difficult also for the audience to understand.

The revised version given in the key is easy to say, easy for you to remember, and easy for your audience to understand.

You can only make your speech easier if you have a script.

3.4 How can I use TED to help me write a script?

Read this transcript below from a TED presentation. The *21 minutes* refer to length of the presentation.

Do you think the presenter will say the words in bold a) more quickly, b) more slowly? Why?

> When you have 21 minutes to **speak**, two million years seems like **a really long time**. But evolutionarily, two million years is nothing. **And yet, in two million years, the human brain has nearly tripled in mass.** Going from the one-and-a-quarter-pound brain of our ancestor here, Habilis, to the almost three-pound meatloaf everybody here has between their ears. **What is it about a big brain that nature was so eager for every one of us to have one?**
>
> Well, it turns out when brains triple in size, they don't just get **three times bigger**. They **gain new structures**. And one of the main reasons our brain got so big is because it got **a new part**, called the "frontal lobe," **particularly, a part called the "prefrontal cortex."** What does a prefrontal cortex **do for you that should justify the entire architectural overhaul of the human skull** in the blink of evolutionary time?
>
> Well, it turns out the prefrontal cortex does **lots of things**, but **one of the most important** things it does is **it's an experience simulator**. Pilots practice in **flight simulators** so that they don't make **real mistakes in planes**. **Human beings** have this marvelous adaptation that they can actually have **experiences in their heads before they try them out** in real life. This is a trick that none of our ancestors could do, and that **no other animal** can do quite like we can.

Now watch up to 01.14 (or more if you are finding it interesting!)

https://www.ted.com/talks/dan_gilbert_the_surprising_science_of_happiness/transcript?language=en

3.4 How can I use TED to help me write a script? (cont.)

1. Did he speak the words in bold more slowly or quickly?
2. In general, did he speak too quickly for you to understand well (try listening to another part, but without the script or subtitles).
3. Below are some statistics on the transcript. How could you use these statistics to help you prepare your script for your presentation?

   Number of words: 236

   Average sentence length: 20 words

   Length in time: 71 seconds

   Words per second: 3.3

   Words per minute: just under 200

1. More slowly. He wants the audience to concentrate on these words. The other words he says much more quickly. The speed of voice helps the audience to understand when they need to listen the most: fast = not so important, slow = very important, please listen carefully.
2. See below.
3. You can compare the statistics with your own script. His phrases are never very long. His average sentence length is 20 words, but all his sentences are divided into shorter parts, and he tends to pause a little between each phrase. So you can aim for a similar length of sentence. For more about this see 2.5.

This presenter speaks fast. I imagine that if you watched without subtitles/script, then you found him difficult to follow. So this means that if you talk at the same speed as him (200 words per minute), most of the audience will probably not understand you.

You should speak at between 140 and 170 words per minute.

Don't try to speak at the speed of a fast native speaker. An audience probably won't have problems with the native presenter's pronunciation, grammar or vocabulary – they only have to manage his/her speed (and perhaps his/her accent).

3.4 How can I use TED to help me write a script? (cont.)

But if YOU speak very fast it will make you seem nervous. If you combine nervousness with your accent, your pronunciation, your intonation and your general level of English, your audience will probably have difficulty understanding you.

Don't worry if your accent, pronunciation and intonation are not perfect. If you articulate each word clearly and speak slowly, the audience will be able to understand you.

Many people in the audience will be non-native speakers like you, so they will certainly appreciate you speaking slowly and clearly. They will probably understand more of what you say than a native speaker who speaks perfect English but at high speed!

You can use your script to calculate how fast you would need to speak. How?

i. Record yourself doing your presentation using Zoom or a similar application.
ii. Note how many minutes it took you.
iii. Calculate the number of words in your speech and divide it by the minutes you took to do your presentation. You will now have your words per minute.

If this number is above 170, you need to think of ways of reducing what you say and possibly reducing the level of detail on your slides.

Not all TED presenters speak so fast – see 2.5.

3.5 How can I make sure my script is perfect from an English point of view?

How good is your English? Underline all the mistakes in the script below. Don't worry about spelling or punctuation. Also think where you could divide up long sentences to make the speech easier to say.

Note that this was a presentation before a board of examiners. The presenter was obliged to introduce himself and give some background information.

> Before the technical presentation of my project, I start telling you something about me: I'm Italian, more specifically I'm from Viareggio, a beautiful seaside town near Pisa, and I'm 26 years old. I'm a biologist: indeed, on the 27th May, I obtained my master degree in Biology applied to Biomedicine from the university of Pisa, after following a one-year internship in CNR laboratories. There, I was able to learn the basic techniques of molecular and cell biology and, above all, I learned how to work in a team.
>
> On 29th June, I sat the entry examination for the PhD in translational medicine, organized by xxx.
>
> The subject of my project for the following three years will be MICAL2, a protein which plays a key role in tumor progression as it is involved in metastasis and neo-angiogenesis. In fact, the reduction of MICAL2, being a protein involved in the control of cytoskeletal plasticity, promotes the mesenchyme-epithelium transition, a phase in which cell motility and its invasiveness decrease, and the cell assumes epithelial characteristics; on the contrary, the over-expression of MICAL2 has been associated with the epithelium-mesenchymatic transition, in gastric and renal tumors, necessary for neoplastic cells to increase the migratory capacity and invade other tissues, generating metastasis.

Below are my corrections to the script. The square brackets indicate parts that I think he could delete. Note how I have divided it into short paragraphs. This makes it much easier for the presenter to read.

How many mistakes did you NOT identify when you did the task above?

3.5 How can I make sure my script is perfect from an English point of view? (cont.)

[[[Before the technical presentation of my project, I would like to start by telling you something about me:]] So I'm ~~italian~~Italian, ~~more specifically I'm~~ from Viareggio, a beautiful seaside town near Pisa~~,~~ ~~and~~ I'm 26 years old.

I'm a biologist~~: indeed, on the 27th May, I obtained my master~~. Earlier this year I finished my Master's ~~degree~~ in Biology applied to Biomedicine from the university of Pisa~~,~~ ~~after~~ During my course ~~following~~ I did a one-year internship ~~in CNR laboratories~~ at the Italian National Research Council. ~~There, I was able to learn~~ I learned the basic techniques of molecular and cell biology ~~and,~~ ~~a~~Above all, learned how to work in a team.

~~On 29th June, I sat the entry examination for the~~ So now I'm doing PhD in translational medicine, organized by xxx.

~~The subject of my project for the following three years will be~~ I am studying **MICAL2**. MICAL2 is~~,~~ a protein which plays a key role in tumor progression. ~~as it~~It is involved in metastasis and neo-angiogenesis. ~~In fact, the reduction of~~ MICAL2~~, being~~ is a protein involved in the control of cytoskeletal plasticity. If MICAL2 is reduced, this~~,~~ promotes the mesenchyme-epithelium transition.~~,~~ This is a good thing because this transition is a phase in which cell motility and its invasiveness decrease, and the cell assumes epithelial characteristics.~~;~~ ~~on~~

However~~the contrary,~~ the over-expression of MICAL2 has been associated with the epithelium-mesenchymatic transition, in gastric and renal tumors. ~~,~~ This epithelium-mesenchymatic transition is very harmful as it ~~necessary~~ means that~~for~~ neoplastic cells ~~to~~ increase their migratory capacity and invade other tissues, generating metastasis.

3.5 How can I make sure my script is perfect from an English point of view? (cont.)

A massive advantage of having a script is that you can email it to a native English speaker to correct it for you. If you don't have a script, it would be much more difficult for a native English speaker to help you.

An English speaker he/she may also be able to suggest ways of improving the script not just from a grammatical point of view. For example, the words in circles are words that I added to make the speech more dramatic and incisive, and to help the audience understand the importance of what the presenter is saying.

3.6 How can I use my script to help me with my pronunciation, intonation and tone?

Let's imagine you begin your presentation in the very typical academic way. The text below is just designed to illustrate how to use a script to help your pronunciation and intonation. I would NOT recommend beginning a presentation like this, instead use one of the strategies suggested in Chapter 6. Which of the suggestions do you think would be most useful for you?

SCRIPT WITH NO ANNOTATIONS

> First of all, thank you very much for coming here today. My name's Jo Smith and I am a researcher at the University of Manchester.

DIVIDE UP INTO SHORT PHRASES TO INDICATE WHERE YOU WANT TO PAUSE (/)

> First of all / thank you very much / for coming here today. My name's Jo Smith / and I am a researcher / at the University of Manchester.

DECIDE WHICH WORDS TO STRESS (bold)

> **First** of all / **thank** you very much / for **coming** here today. My name's **Jo Smith** / and I am a **researcher** / the **University** of **Manchester**.

LEARN INDIVIDUAL WORD STRESS (underline)

> Let me just <u>out</u>line what I'll be dis<u>cuss</u>ing today. First, I'm going to tell you / something about the <u>back</u>ground to this work. Then I'll take a **brief look** at the re<u>la</u>ted <u>lit</u>erature / and the <u>meth</u>ods we used. Finally, and most im<u>por</u>tantly, I'll show you our **key** re<u>sults</u>.

USE EXTRA STRESS TO SHOW STRUCTURE (bold + underline)

> Let me just outline what I'll be discussing today. **<u>First</u>**, I'm going to tell you something about the background to this work. **<u>Then</u>** I'll take a brief look at the related literature and the methods we used. **<u>Finally</u>**, and most importantly, I'll show you our key results.

3.6 How can I use my script to help me with my pronunciation, intonation and tone? (cont.)

Submit your speech to Google Translate (4.4). Listen to it and follow the speaker's voice carefully. Note the words they stress, and what parts of the sentence they stress the most.

Annotate your own script using the annotations outlined above or any other ones that you find easy and useful.

Read your script aloud and record it.

Listen again to your recording. Does it coincide with the Google Translate version? Decide if you need to change anything: the way you speak or what you have annotated.

You can then use you final annotated speech to practise wherever you are.

Alternatively, get a native speaker to annotate your speech and record it for you.

3.7 How should I format/print my script?

Look at the three formats (A, B, C) on the next page. You don't need to read the text. Imagine you had to choose one of these formats to enable you to check and edit your script. Which is easiest to read on your screen?

1. Which is easiest to edit directly on your screen?
2. Which is easiest to read and/or edit when printed?

3.7 How should I format/print my script? (cont.)

A

We investigated a series of selfish behaviors to understand whether they are more frequently shown by big-enders (BEs) and small-enders (SEs), and what the consequent implications are on community living. We also compared these behaviors with right-handers and left-handers, i.e. people with a propensity to use one hand rather than the other to break their eggs. Other authors have studied selfish behavior of BEs and SEs in relation to level of income (Dosh et al, 2020), level of education and critical thinking (Schule et al, 2019), intelligence quotient and cognitive dissonance (Iqbal & Mensa, 2025), musical taste (Hamonija, 2026), taste in movies (Flix & Odeon, 2027), and historical tyrants (Des Pott et al, 2028). However, in all cases the sample sizes were relatively small - education (501 subjects), IQ (145), music (88), movies (345), and tyrants (29). Our sample was approximately 10,000 people spread over three continents (N. America, Europe and Asia). In fact, to the best of our knowledge our sample is the largest ever used in a psycho-social study of endedness, where 'endedness' is defined as the tendency to break an egg at one end more frequently than the other end.

B

We investigated a series of selfish behaviors to understand whether they are more frequently shown by big-enders (BEs) and small-enders (SEs), and what the consequent implications are on community living. We also compared these behaviors with right-handers and left-handers, i.e. people with a propensity to use one hand rather than the other to break their eggs. Other authors have studied selfish behavior of BEs and SEs in relation to level of income (Dosh et al, 2020), level of education and critical thinking (Schule et al, 2019), intelligence quotient and cognitive dissonance (Iqbal & Mensa, 2025), musical taste (Hamonija, 2026), taste in movies (Flix & Odeon, 2027), and historical tyrants (Des Pott et al, 2028). However, in all cases the sample sizes were relatively small - education (501 subjects), IQ (145), music (88), movies (345), and tyrants (29).

C

We investigated a series of selfish behaviors to understand whether they are more frequently shown by big-enders (BEs) and small-enders (SEs), and what the consequent implications are on community living. We also compared these behaviors with right-handers and left-handers, i.e. people with a propensity to use one hand rather than the other to break their eggs. Other authors have studied selfish behavior of BEs and SEs in relation to level of income (Dosh et al, 2020), level of education and critical thinking (Schule et al, 2019), intelligence quotient and cognitive dissonance (Iqbal & Mensa, 2025), musical taste (Hamonija, 2026), taste in movies (Flix & Odeon, 2027), and historical tyrants (Des Pott et al, 2028). However, in all cases the sample sizes were relatively small - education (501 subjects), IQ (145), music (88), movies (345), and tyrants (29).

3.7 How should I format/print my script? (cont.)

How you format your script (or your manuscript, or any document) makes a big difference to how easily and efficiently you will be able to read it, edit it, and look for mistakes.

A) This is Times New Roman (10pt), which many people use by default. This font is used in many textbooks, including this one. However, it is generally more difficult to read and edit on a screen. It is even more difficult, if, as in the screenshot on the previous page, there is single line spacing and right-hand justification (red circle in the screenshot below):

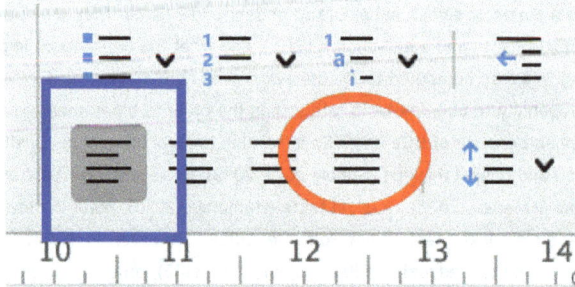

B) This is Arial (10 pt). It is has double interlining and is justified to the left only (blue square in the screenshot).

C) This is Calibri (12 pt). It is formatted the same as B), but the margins are wider and it is in 12pt. The text thus occupies less space on each line and each word is bigger given the bigger font size. This tends to make it easier to read.

I would suggest using whatever font you find the easiest to read, but always use double space lining, and do not justify to the right (only to the left).

3.8 Using Google Translate to translate your script

If you don't speak very good English, then a good option is to write your script in your own language and then use Google Translate (GT), or alternatively DeepL.

Here is a good procedure to follow.

STAGE 1

1. Talk to friends or family about your research.
2. Note what they find interesting and also what they find difficult to understand.
3. Produce a first draft in your own language.
4. Practise this draft with fellow students but preferably not of your discipline. Get them to give you feedback and also to ask you questions.
5. Incorporate into your script: i) their feedback, and ii) the answers to any useful questions they asked.
6. Produce a final script in your own language that you are happy with.

STAGE 2

Go through the script and analyse it as if you were going to write it in English:

- Make every sentence as short as possible. But vary the length of sentences. They should not all be too short.
- Make sure you always use the most specific word possible.
- Ensure that you follow this word order: Subject Verb Object, and that these three elements are as close as possible together.
- Replace words such as *it, them, these, those,* with the words that they refer to. This will make it easier for your audience understand what you are referring to.

3.8 Using Google Translate to translate your script (cont.)

Through the guidelines you will learn how to:

- prepare/modify your text in your own language so that you considerably improve the chances of GT doing an accurate translation
- avoid the typical mistakes you make when writing directly into English
- spot mistakes that GT makes

The document also sections on:

- how to use the Spelling and Editor functions of Microsoft Word
- websites and applications that will help you CHECK (rather than translate) your English

English for Presentations at International Conferences, Chapter 3, gives full details on how to write a script, including grammar issues and how to be concise.

Chapter 4
Pronunciation, intonation, and speed of voice

4.1 Why do I need to improve my pronunciation?

Which of these ten words are you 100% sure that you pronounce correctly?

1. architecture
2. diagnosis
3. hello
4. hierarchy
5. management
6. parameter
7. report (noun and verb)
8. through
9. force
10. worse

Check using Google Translate (see 4.4). As you listen to 1-7, underline where the stress falls (e.g. communi*ca*tion, *Eng*lish). For 8, listen how the *th* is pronounced. For 9 and 10 listen and see if *force* and *worse* have an identical pronunciation apart from the initial consonant.

archi*tec*ture (the 'ch' has a 'k' sound)

dia*gno*sis (the *g* and *n* have a separate sound; they are not merged into one sound. Similar words are: magnetic, signature)

he*llo* (only one L is pronounced)

*hie*rarchy (*hie* is pronounce liked *high,* the 'ch' has a 'k' sound)

*man*agement (the '*age*' is pronounced like the *idge* in fr*idge*)

pa*ra*meter

4.1 Why do I need to improve my pronunciation? (cont.)

re*port* (noun and verb)

through (same pronunciation as *true*, but with a *th* at the beginning)

force (the *or* is pronounced like *oor* in *door*), worse (the *or* is pronounced like the *er* in *her*)

If you mispronounce key words, your audience might be confused.

But don't worry. Your presentation will not contain many words that you cannot already pronounce (see 4.2). Using online applications (see 4.4) is not difficult to learn how to pronounce this limited number of words. Speak slowly and articulate clearly: even if you make some pronunciation mistakes, the audience will probably still understand you.

On YouTube you can find various tutorials on pronunciation to help you, for example, position your tongue correctly to obtain the *th* sound, and to distinguish between the two pronunciations of *th* (*this* vs *those*). In this case, just search for 'th sound'.

To learn how you sound, record yourself.

English for Interacting on Campus Chapter 10 Pronunciation

4.2 How many words will I have to learn how to pronounce correctly?

A typical ten-minute presentation requires around 1500 words, most of which are repeated several times, e.g. common words such *as a, an, the, at, in, be, was, large, small, start, finish, diagram, slide*

1. What percentage of these 1500 words do you think you can already pronounce correctly because they are words from general English (i.e. not technical words)?

a) 10% b) 50% c) 80%

2. Your presentation will contain key words relating to your research area. What percentage of your key words do you think you already pronounce correctly?

a) 20% b) 50% c) 90%

3. So, how many words in your presentation do you think you need to learn to pronounce correctly because at the moment you are not totally sure of their pronunciation?

Technical words: a) 5-10 b) 11-25 c) 26-50) d) 51-100

Non-technical words: a) 5-10 b) 11-25 c) 26-50) d) 51-100

This key is based on the total number of words, including repetitions of the same word. For example, the words *a/an, the* and *and* may be repeated as many as 45, 70 and 150 times, respectively, in a total of 1500 words. Incredibly, *and* can account for around 10% of all the words used! These statistics are based on transcripts of TED presentations, which tend to be less technical than academic presentations. The proportion of non-key words is thus likely to be higher in a TED presentation than in your presentation, but the numbers are still indicative.

1) Non-key words make up the basis of the presentation, representing at least 80% of the entire words.

2) Based on my lessons with PhD students, I would say that they already know how to pronounce around 95% of the words in their speech.

3) Again, based on my teaching experience, you probably only mispronounce a total of 10 words in your speech (probably more non-key words than key words).

4.3 Will my accent interfere with the audience's understanding of my English? What other factors might prevent the audience from understanding me?

1. In your country, which regional accents are the a) easiest, b) the most difficult to understand? Why?
2. Which accents of non-native speakers of your language do you find most difficult to understand? Why?
3. How good is the English accent of people from your country? What problems do they / you typically have?
4. Do you think that your English accent will stop the audience from understanding you?

An accent, however strong, is NOT important if it does not:

- interfere with the audience's understanding
- does not annoy / disturb the audience in some way

For me, accent is generally NOT a key part of mispronunciation. I am English and I have lived in Italy for 35 years, but still speak Italian with an English accent. I don't sound like an Italian, but people understand me perfectly.

What really stops an audience from understanding your English or becoming annoyed by your pronunciation, is possibly because you:

- Put the stress on the wrong part of the word. For example, *interESTing* rather than *INteresting*. Generally speaking this does not interfere with the audience's understanding of the word. However, it may become irritating for the audience if you continually put the stress in the wrong place on a word. If the audience is distracted by your pronunciation, then they will listen less attentively.

- Mispronounce a vowel sound. For example, saying *forced* when you mean *first*. This will certainly confuse the audience. It is a key priority that you learn how to pronounce such words correctly,

- Mispronounce a consonant. For example, saying *tank* rather than *thank*. This kind of mistake may sound funny to the audience – thus distracting them. On other occasions, it may prevent them from understanding.

- Use acronyms. The letters of the alphabet are pronounced in different ways in different languages. Consequently, acronyms are often difficult for the audience to process. It is thus better to say the full words rather than just their initial letters.

4.4 How can I check my pronunciation without the help of a teacher?

Type a text of around 50 words describing some of the difficulties you have with English pronunciation. Alternatively, copy a paragraph from this book.

Now paste your text into the appropriate boxes of the websites below. Decide which website you like best and why.

URL	DESCRIPTION
https://ttsdemo.com/	Text-to-speech website, also known as Oddcast.
https://translate.google.com/	A translation site, but you can also i) type in lists of words, ii) upload documents (e.g. your script). You can then listen to the lists and the documents.
https://www.deepl.com/translator	Same comments as above for Google Translate.

These sites are excellent if you want to hear how your speech sounds.

As you listen, highlight the words that are pronounced in a different way from what you expected. You will need to repeat this task several times in order to identify these words.

You can then compile a list of these words and practise them with the help of the four sites given on the next page.

By inserting and listening to your whole speech, you should also be able to understand which sentences are too long or would be difficult for you to say.

You can also identify which words you cannot pronounce. This means that you can find synonyms for non-key words and thus replace words that are difficult to pronounce with words that are easier. For example, you can replace:

- a multi-syllable word, such as *innovative,* with a monosyllable word e.g. *new*
- a word with a difficult consonant sound such as, *usually* or *thesis*, with a word that does not contain that sound, e.g. *often*, *paper*
- a word with a difficult vowel sound, such as *worldwide*, with a word that has an easier vowel sound, e.g. *globally*

4.4 How can I check my pronunciation without the help of a teacher? (cont.)

Make a list of 5-10 words that you find difficult to pronounce. Now use the following sites to check the pronunciation. What, if any, are the differences between how sites are organized? In addition to pronunciation, what else can you learn from these sites?

https://howjsay.com/

https://www.learnersdictionary.com/

https://www.oxfordlearnersdictionaries.com/

https://www.wordreference.com/

When you listen to lists of words using Google Translate or the other text-to-speech sites, you can use this trick for slowing the speaker down. Follow the steps below:

1. Type in your list.
2. Hit the sound icon (circled in read in the screenshot below). You will hear the words said at a normal speed.
3. Hit the sound icon again. The words are said more slowly.

4.4 How can I check my pronunciation without the help of a teacher? (cont.)

However, if you want the speaker to speak really slowly, put a full stop after each word. This makes the speaker think that this is the end of the sentence, so the speaker pauses for longer between each word.

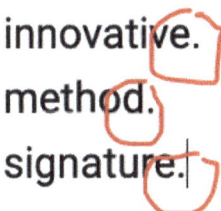

innovative.
method.
signature.

With this system you can note:

i) which syllable in a word is stressed (is it *INnovative*, *innNOVative*, or *innoVAtive*?)

ii) the vowel sound (is the 'e' sound in *method* pronounced like *met* or *meet*?)

iii) whether a consonant is silent or not (is the *g* in *signature* like the g in *sign*?)

i) *INnovative* or *innoVAtive* – both are possible, although until recently only the first was the 'official' pronunciation.

ii) *met* in *method*, *meet* in *methane*

iii) in *signature* the *g* and *n* are both sounded separately: *sig na ture*. In *sign*, the *g* is silent.

4.5 Subtitling. How can I check how well a native audience will understand my pronunciation?

The screenshots in this section are the opening slide from one of my lectures on the problems of ambiguity.

The screenshot below shows how to use subtitles in Microsoft PowerPoint.

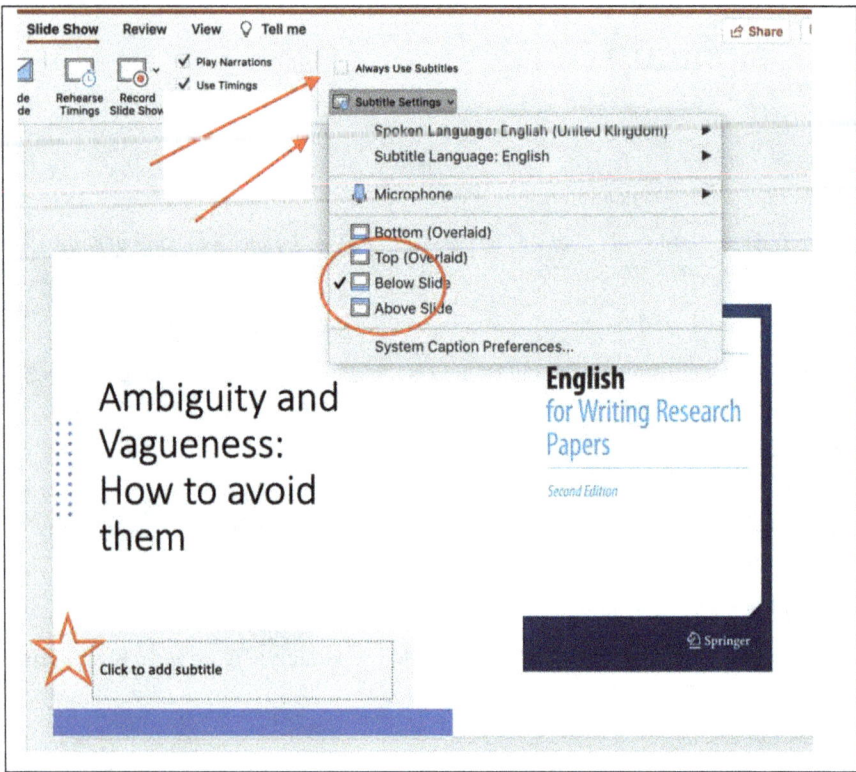

- Open your presentation
- Select Slide Slow from the top menu.
- Click *Always Use Subtitles*
- Choose the language.
- Choose the position where you want the subtitles to appear.
- Start your slide show using Full Screen.

4.5 Subtitling. How can I check how well a native audience will understand my pronunciation? (cont.)

- Talk from your script (see Chapter 3) and subtitles will appear.
- Finally, compare the subtitles with what you read from your speech. If they don't match, then you need to improve your pronunciation. You can do a similar test using the Dictate function from Microsoft Word:

Dictate

Now look back at the screenshot on the previous page. Look at the bottom which I have marked with a red star ('Click to add subtitle'). If you want, you can insert your own subtitles, i.e. you can cut & paste from your script. An example is shown below (the circle in red is the subtitles):

Ambiguity and Vagueness: How to avoid them

This is what I am going to say.

4.5 Subtitling. How can I check how well a native audience will understand my pronunciation? (cont.)

The screenshot below shows the location and appearance of the subtitles when you are giving your presentation live, i.e. you haven't already pre-written the subtitles.

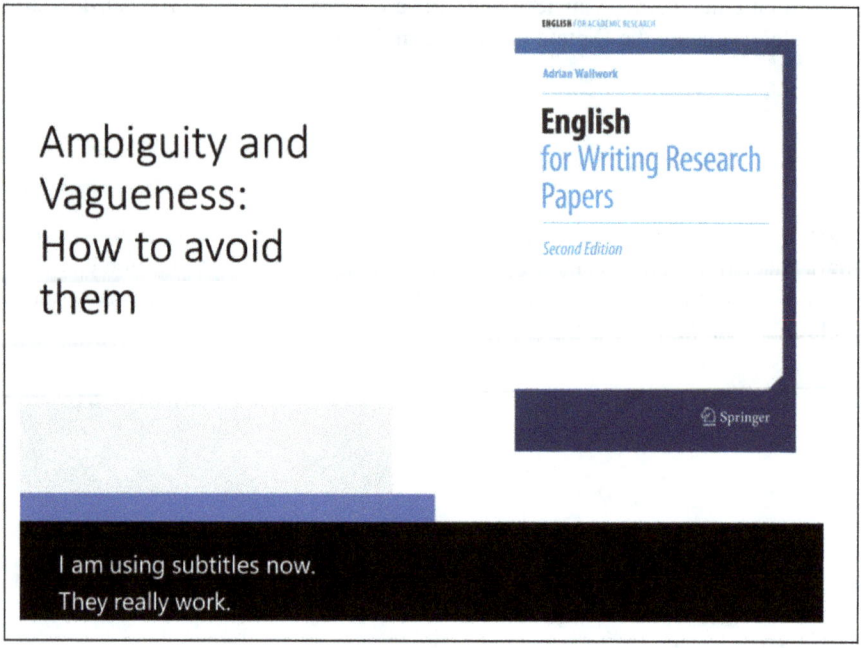

If you are pre-recording your presentation and you have prepared a script (see Chapter 3), then using subtitles is an excellent way to:

- ensure that everyone can understand what you have said
- help those whose level of English is not as good as yours and may find it helpful to read your subtitles rather than listen to you speak.

When movies are subtitled (e.g. an English movie with English subtitles), they do not usually report every word that is said, but just a short version. You can do the same: just have a short version of what you say.

In any case, when you write your script (see Chapter 3), you should already try to write in short sentences.

4.6 When speaking, what kinds of words do I need to pay special attention to?

Some words are more important for the audience to understand than others. Below is a list of three areas where you need to take more trouble to pronounce the words correctly.

NUMBERS

Distinguish clearly between 13 and 30, 14 and 40, etc. Note where the stress is: *thirteen thirty*. Make sure you clearly enunciate the *n* in *thirteen, fourteen* etc. You can help your audience by writing important numbers directly onto your slides.

ENGLISH TECHNICAL WORDS THAT ALSO EXIST IN YOUR LANGUAGE

Say your key words and English technical words more slowly.

Some English technical words and acronyms (and abbreviations) are also found in many other languages: *lockdown, hardware; PC, CEO, ID*

In your language, English words may be pronounced in a different way from a native English speaker. So it is a good idea to the learn the 'correct' pronunciation, otherwise the audience may not understand you.

- Words consisting of two words have the stress in English on the first syllable: *ha*r*dware, su*permarket, *mo*bile phone

- Words whose second part is a preposition also have the stress on the first syllable: *back* up, *log* in

- letters in acronyms have equal stress: *P-C, C-E-O*

-*ED* ENDINGS

When you add -*ed* to form the past forms of a verb, you do not add an extra syllable. For example the verbs *focused, followed, informed* are NOT pronounced *focus sed, follow wed, inform med*. The number of syllables of a verb in its infinitive form (*fo cus*) and in its past form (*fo cust*, spelled *focused*) is the same. The only exceptions are verbs whose infinitive form ends in -*d* or -*t*, for example *added, painted*, which are pronounced *add did* and *paint tid*. Mispronouncing the -*ed* will NOT confuse the audience, but it may distract them.

4.7 I am very worried that my audience will not understand my English pronunciation. Which sounds do I not need to worry about?

When you are giving a presentation, you are likely to be nervous about your English pronunciation. It may help you to know that there are some areas of pronunciation that are NOT very important. Some examples are listed below.

US VS UK PRONUNCIATIONS

There are many words that are pronounced in different ways between American and British English.

Examples: *address, adult, detail, frustrated, router, twenty*

Given that these differences don't usually cause problems between Americans and Brits, then you don't need to worry about them. The important thing is that your pronunciation is standard (or as standard as possible). It does not matter which standard you use.

TH

Many native speakers pronounce *th* sound as if it was a *d, t* or *f*. So *thing* becomes: *ding, ting, fing*! So if native speakers can mispronounce words that begin with TH, so can you!

MULTISYLLABLE WORDS

Examples of multisyllable words: *difficult, photographic, chemical, kilometer, contribute*

Because multisyllable words are long, the audience has more time to hear them (and identify them). So if you say *inteRESting* instead of *INtresting*, your audience will still understand you.

In any case, amongst native speakers there is often more than one acceptable pronunciation of particular words. So native speakers may say: *CONtribute* and *conTRIBute*, *KILometer* and *kiLOMeter*. However, they will only say *paRAMeter* and not *paraMEter*.

4.7 I am very worried that my audience will not understand my English pronunciation. Which sounds do I not need to worry about? (cont.)

When you have practised your presentation many times, ask an English teacher to listen to you giving your presentation. The teacher should write down every word that you pronounce incorrectly, and then teach you the correct pronunciation. You will not need more than a couple of lessons and you can easily find such teachers online. Online works very well because you can really see the teacher's mouth, lips and tongue which will help you to understand how to 'make' the sound.

Speak slowly and enunciate clearly. Even if your pronunciation is 'terrible', by speaking slowly and articulating each word the audience will have a greater chance of understanding you. They will, however, have difficulty if you speak fast without pauses (which is typical if you are nervous).

Chapter 5
Titles

5.1 What is the purpose of the title slide of a presentation?

1. Think of three reasons why your title slide is important.
2. What is its purpose?
3. How technical should it be?
4. What kinds of audience is the title slide designed to attract?

When choosing your title:

- Imagine that your research is a product that you are trying to sell to the audience. The title of your presentation is a like an advertisement for your product.
- Don't automatically use the title of your thesis or paper. It is probably too technical to be the title of your presentation.
- Remember that not all your audience will be experts in your field. Some people may be from other fields who are interested to see if there is any common ground with your field. By attracting this kind of audience you increase the chances of interesting multi-disciplinary collaborations (see 1.1).

Find four title slides from presentations in your field of research given at international conferences.

1. Put them in order of preference (1 = the one you like the most, 4 = the least).
2. Analyse the one you like the least – what problems does it have?
3. Analyse the one you like the most – what makes it better than the others?

5.2 How important are key words in my title?

When you are drafting your presentation, think about the key words that you want to include. Write the key words in a vertical list. Look at your list and rank them according to how important they are. You should then try and locate the most important key word as near as possible to the beginning of the title.

Below are four versions of a presentation on how companies similar to Amazon plan the routes of their drivers in order to be able to deliver packages on the same day (as promised to Amazon Prime customers).

Note how the position of various key words (in bold) directs the audience's attention regarding what the focus of the presentation will be. Which do you personally think is the best / most specific?

> An **optimization algorithm** for planning routes to solve the same-day delivery problem.
>
> **Same day deliveries**: an optimization algorithm for planning routes
>
> **Planning routes** for same-day deliveries: an optimization algorithm
>
> **Route planning** for same-day deliveries: an optimization algorithm

There is no correct answer, it depends where the focus of the presentation is. However, by themselves, none of the titles are particularly attractive.

Below is a title that might appeal to a wider audience. Many people in the audience will have used Amazon (or a courier service).

5.2 How important are key words in my title? (cont.)

Below are a series of titles for a conference. Don't worry, they are very technical, and you are unlikely to understand them. However, you can probably differentiate between the more generic words and the very technical / scientific words. For each title, see if you can do either one or both of the following:

a) relocate key words to the beginning

b) reduce the title by two words or more

1. A computational approach to the exploitation of glutamine as an infrared probe for a greater understanding of the local environment properties of fibril structures:

2. A novel investigation into the modeling of the Resonance Raman spectroscopies of Doxorubicin-DNA complexes

3. The adsorption energies and main spectroscopic properties of N-Methylformamide on a TiO2 anatase surface.

1. Glutamine as an infrared probe to understand local environment properties of fibril structures: a computational approach

2. Using XYZ* to model Resonance Raman spectroscopies of Doxorubicin-DNA complexes

3. N-Methylformamide on a TiO2 anatase surface: adsorption energies and main spectroscopic properties

* where XYZ stands for a specific technical procedure.

5.3 I like very simple title slides with no images – to me they seem more professional. Is this a good approach?

Look at the title below.

> *Development and production of*
>
> *a Controlled Release Fertilizer*
>
> Name of presenter

1. Do you understand the title? What is a *controlled release fertilizer*?
2. Does every word have a purpose? Could some words be deleted?
3. Does the slide look professional?
4. Does it look like the presenter made a big effort to produce an aesthetically pleasing slide (i.e. a nice-looking slide)?
5. Will the slide attract the attention of the audience?

1) The title gives very little information. What is a *controlled release fertilizer*? What is the fertilizer for? Why is a controlled release important? How did they develop the fertilizer? Is it successful? Where has it been applied?

   Clearly your title cannot answer all these questions, but it has to be as specific as possible.

2) There is redundancy: what value does 'Development and production of' give to the audience?

3) No. It does nothing to enhance the credibility of the presenter.

4) It may give the impression it took 20 seconds to prepare and highlights that presenter doesn't really care about the audience. Or it simply shows a lack of imagination.

5) No.

5.3 I like very simple title slides with no images – to me they seem more professional. Is this a good approach? (cont.)

Look at the slide below, which gives a much better overall picture of the presentation.

This slide also enables the presenter to give a very quick summary of what he/she is going to talk about as all the key words are either in the title or will be given when he describes the images.

The topic of the presentation is the development of a new controlled-release fertilizer, which is obtained from leftovers and waste produced by the agri-food sector (such as the coffee powder that remains when a cup of coffee has been produced in a coffee making machine). You can see the waste products on the left of the slide. These are then used to produce pellets (image in the middle of the slide). These pellets are then used to fertilize plants (right-hand image). The pellets release nutrients over a long period of time, hence 'controlled release'. This kind of recycling of waste products is called the 'circular economy' (i.e. minimizing waste and pollution, and reusing products and materials as many times as possible).

However the title has left out a key element of the underlying concept of this presenter's research: the circular economy. So an even better title would be:

> A slow-releasing fertilizer using clay, coffee and
> agri-food waste: a circular economist's dream

5.4 I am a researcher in the Humanities / Arts. How can I make my title more specific?

Analyse the titles below.

- Which ones seem the most specific?
- Which ones contain the vaguest words / phrases?

a) The foreign policy of Ferdinando I de' Medici (1587-1609)

b) Power or exploitation? Beyond a false alternative in social philosophy

c) Feminist movements and the production of safer spaces in an urban context

d) Organizing a protest without organizations: The defense of the voting stations during the 2017 independence referendum in Catalonia

e) Whistleblowing from below: how civil society actors influence the implementation of anti-corruption policies through digital media

The most specific are d) and e).

You may think that a) is specific. But if you were at a conference of historians this title would tell you very little. What about the foreign policy? The audience want to know some details about what is new about what this researcher has found. Do the dates refer to Ferdinando's birth and death, or the period of his foreign policy?

b) What does this title mean? *Power or exploitation* of what? What is *a false alternative* and how does one go *beyond* it? This is the kind of title that sounds good, but has little substance.

c) *Feminist movements*: when and where? *Safer spaces* – for example? Does *in an urban context* simply mean 'in towns'? If so, in all parts of the town, or just in some?

Don't underestimate the importance of your title. Many people will decide to come to your presentation purely based on the title. If the title makes no sense or is so generic that it gives no clue regarding the content, then some people will decide not to attend. You have thus wasted a huge opportunity.

5.5 Does my title have to be the first slide? Can I put my title in the second or third slide?

Below are the first five slides of a presentation about what the general public (civil society) can do to oppose something; for example, the building of a nuclear power plant in their local area. The presenter is from a country where it is difficult to organize opposition.

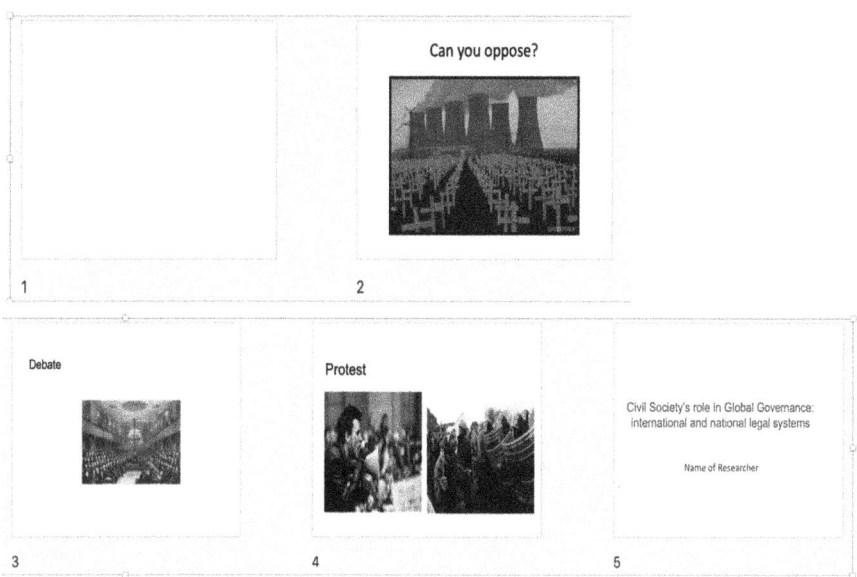

Her solution is explained in the five points below which refer to the five slides in the screenshot.

1. begin with a blank screen – this is guaranteed to get audience attention, it is not what the audience are expecting to see

2. immediately ask the audience a question: *Imagine your government wants to build a nuclear power plant near your house. Would you want to stop it? How would you try to stop it?* The idea is to get the audience thinking about opposition rights in their country

3. say how opposition is dealt with in the UK and the USA, i.e. democratically through parliament (ideally!)

5.5 Does my title have to be the first slide? Can I put my title in the second or third slide? (cont.)

4. show what happens in her country: demonstrations of the people vs the police [in reality this happens in the UK and USA too!]
5. the title slide: *Civil Society's role in Global Governance: International and national legal systems*

A good way to think about whether it might be a good idea not to have your title slide as your first slide is to use the 'slide sorter' (see 9.1) in your presentation software. This will also help you to decide what slides you could delete.

5.6 What is essential to include in my title slide? And what can I leave out to create a cleaner slide?

There is no standard way to construct a title slide, but most presenters prioritize information by using different font sizes. The two most important elements, which should be given the most space, are:

1. the title
2. your name

   Other things that some presenters sometimes include are:

3. the name and date of the conference (this helps in web searches)
4. co-authors
5. the name and/or logo of your institute/research unit
6. your supervisor
7. acknowledgments
8. sponsors
9. a photo
10. a background image

Some of the best presenters use their title slide to attract audience attention. They do this either by completely ignoring points 3–7 above, or by putting such details in a very small font. Points 3–7 generally contain no information that 99.9% of the audience need to know or that they can't find out from the conference program.

Point 3 has become a kind of standard way to show that the presentation is not simply a recycled version of a previous one—this goes to the extent of putting the conference name and date on every single slide. This seems totally unnecessary.

Points 4–7 tend to be included exclusively to satisfy colleagues, professors, supervisors, and those that have helped during your research. It probably makes more sense to thank these people face to face. If you are part of a research team, there is no need to list all the names of the people in your team. If you absolutely must give acknowledgments to such people, then it is probably a good idea to put their names in a small font and in a non-prominent position in your title slide (or in your last slide). Similarly, if you have participated in many projects, you don't need to write the names of these projects. This kind of information is very pertinent to you, but it is usually of no interest to the audience. You could simply say, "*There are 14 people in our team and we have already participated in 10 projects.*" That is all the audience needs to know.

5.6 What is essential to include in my title slide? And what can I leave out to create a cleaner slide? (cont.)

Point 8 you may have a contractual obligation to mention sponsors.

Points 9 and 10 may help to make your title slide look more interesting. Typical photos and background images include elements of your research or photos (or maps) from your country of origin.

The more information you have on your title slide the more it will detract away from the most important things: your title and your name.

This section comes from 4.2.4 of *English for Presentations at International Conferences*.

For more on writing titles see Chapter 12 in *English for Writing Research Papers*.

Make a pencil draft of your title. Think about:

- A two-part heading: i) non-technical ii) technical
- Location of title and your name
- A clear impactful and relevant image
- Other information to include: institute logos, sponsor logos, names of other people

Then 'add notes' about what you would say.

5.6 What is essential to include in my title slide? And what can I leave out to create a cleaner slide? (cont.)

Typical mistakes made when writing titles

2, 3, 94-96, *100 Tips to Avoid Mistakes in Academic Writing and Presenting*

Advanced guidelines on writing titles

4.2, *English for Presentations at International Conferences*

Chapter 12, *English for Writing Research Papers*

Chapter 6
Starting your presentation: giving the big picture

6.1 What is the most important thing I need to know about how to start my presentation?

When a friend introduces you to someone new at a party, how attentive are you to what your friend says about this person?

Many presenters seem to begin their presentation assuming that the audience:

- is 100% focused on them
- is somehow already totally in tune with them and their research
- is ready for details immediately

So they begin as if the audience were already fully immersed in the topic.

This is rarely the case.

When you are introduced by a friend to someone new, you probably are not concentrating fully on what is being said. Instead you are getting a visual impression of the new person. Your brain is distracted by so much new information that it fails to register the key information – the person's name (or their job, or why your friend thinks that you might have something in common with this new person).

At the beginning of a presentation at a conference, good presenters are aware that their audience is probably thinking about one of more of the following: the previous presentation, what they had for lunch, who the person is that is sitting next to them or in the row behind, the text message they have just received, a phone call they have forgotten to make ... Not all the audience will immediately be focusing on you.

6.1 What is the most important thing I need to know about how to start my presentation? (cont.)

In my experience of having seen thousands of academic presentations, I find that most audiences prefer at the start of presentations to hear about the "big picture" underlying your research. The big picture means the context of your research that explains why you are doing your research. The audience is not ready to immediately hear and digest the details of what you have done. You can create a big picture in many ways, which are outlined in 6.3. Giving the audience the big picture is a way to make them feel more relaxed and to ease them into your presentation.

6.2 How do researchers typically start their presentation? Is this the best way?

The eight introductions (a-h) below come from presentations all given on the same morning of the same conference. The presenters were either PhD students or full-time researchers.

I have only changed the names (NNN) of the presenters, their institutes (XXX), and their locations (LLL). I have not corrected the English, so you will find mistakes.

1. How typical are they of the kind of introductions you often hear at conferences?
2. How similar are they to how you introduce yourself and your presentation?
3. What do they all have in common?
4. What parts would you remove? Why?
5. How attentive do you think the audience will be by the time they hear the sixth or seventh presentation?
6. How captivating is this kind of introduction? Is there an alternative? If so, what?
7. What do the audience really want to hear in an introduction?

a) Good morning everyone. I'm NNN, a researcher of XXX. I am from LLL. I'll present you the last work that I have made in collaboration with my boss, Dr NNN. The title of my work is ...
b) Good morning. I am a PhD student and you are the first people who listen to me speak in a conference. So I apologize for any inconvenience could happening.
c) Good morning. I come from XXX of LLL. I am a contract researcher and my field of research is the study of the relationship between the environment and health. I study ....
d) Good morning all. I would like to tanks all to come her to hear my presentation and tanks to ... for this opportunity. I am NNN and I work at the XXX ... I will talk about ...
e) Good morning everybody. I am very glad to have this opportunity to give my thesis presentations to you on this beautiful morning. Before I start my report I want to show my great honor to you, all the professors, specialists ... and to thank you very much for your coming and attention. The topic of my presentation is ...
f) Good morning all, thank you very much to be here. I am NNN and I work at the institute of XXX. My principal topic is ... and I'm going to talk about ...
g) Good morning to everyone. I'm ... and I'm here to explain about my last work. I hope that any exposition don't be too boring for you and thank you very much

6.2 How do researchers typically start their presentation? Is this the best way? (cont.)

for your presence and interest about my work. So, the subject of this discussion is...

h) The title of my research is: "Consume locally, act globally. A comparative analysis of ecological practices of climate protesters in Italy and France". My research focuses on climate protests started in 2018 after the school strikes promoted by Greta Thunberg in Sweden.

a) c) f) Your name, where you work, and who your supervisor / collaborators are, is generally of little interest to your audience. Your name should obviously be written on your slide, but you don't need to SAY it.

b) g) Don't begin by saying something negative about yourself or about your presentation, this may give the audience a negative expectation.

d) e) Unless you are the only invited speaker there is no need to thank anyone. Also, make sure you pronounce words correctly (thanks, not 'tanks').

h) Never start by reading the title of your presentation. EXPLAIN the title, don't read it.

The way academic presentations are introduced is often uninspiring. The examples given above (a-h) are quite standard, but will not capture the audience's attention. In fact, they may do exactly the opposite. The audience hears words that they have heard so many times before that they stop listening.

Ideally, you want to be remembered so that people will want to contact you. To stand out from the other presenters, you need to find a different way to start your presentation. This different way includes thinking about whether:

1. saying *good morning / afternoon, my name is ...* is necessary and will attract audience attention, or whether you could begin without any salutation or introduction

2. reading aloud the title of your presentation has any purpose, or whether you can just let the audience read it for themselves

3. your title must appear in your first slide, or whether you could perhaps have a first slide that is more eye-catching

6.3 What are some good ways to start a presentation?

Some of the best, or certainly most enjoyable, presentations are those where the presenter simply chats to the audience and / or tries to connect with them immediately.

You can do this by using one or more of the following techniques:

1. give a clear example in the first or second slide that encapsulates the whole meaning of the presentation and immediately gives the audience a context that they can relate to personally. The example probably works best if it is visually appealing

2. say something topical which relates with what you want to say

3. give the audience some very interesting information (statistics)

4. ask a question that contains a counterintuitive or surprising answer (6.4)

5. say something personal about yourself – how you first became interested in the topic, what you particularly like about this area of research, a particular event that took place during the research (e.g. an unexpected problem, an unexpected result). Your aim is to show the audience your enthusiasm for the topic

6. say why you think the audience will be interested in what you are going to say

All the techniques above are useful if you have a diverse audience – i.e. when NOT all the audience is doing exactly the same type of research as you.

Techniques 4-6 are even good when the audience is essentially doing the same research, particularly No. 5 because the audience will naturally compare what you say with their own experience.

You may think that these techniques are just optional. However, it is fundamental to connect with the audience. If you don't connect with them, they will not give you the attention you deserve.

If your presentation is scheduled just before lunch, after lunch or at the end of the day, then you MUST use one of the techniques, otherwise the audience may even fall asleep!

It is a good idea to have alternative beginnings to your presentation. For example, if you have decided to open your presentation with a question, but many of the previous presenters have used the same technique, then your question will lose its power. So you need to have an alternative, such as interesting statistic.

For other methods of beginning your presentation see Chapter 6 Ten Ways to Begin a Presentation in *English for Presentations at International Conferences*.

6.4 What kinds of questions can I ask my audience at the beginning of my presentation?

Look at the following questions. Which ones would work well to open a presentation (i.e. to be the first thing that a presenter says)?

1. In a group of 23 PhD students, how many will have the same birthday?
2. How long does it take to count to one million?
3. Which type of cancer causes the most deaths?
4. Why do people believe in conspiracy theories?
5. Do you know what the term 'cognitive dissonance' means?
6. How many of you take a shower at least once a day?
7. Can you think of five reasons why we should all stop eating meat?

How do you feel if you can't answer a presenter's (or a teacher's / professor's) question? Or if you don't even understand the question?

Questions are an excellent way to gain an audience's attention. However, you need to follow some basic rules.

a) Make your questions easy to answer. Q1-3 are interesting but the audience is unlikely to be able to quickly calculate the answers to Q1 and Q2. So you need to help them. For Q1, you could put the question on a slide (see below), leave the audience a few seconds to read it, and then give them the answer (50 b, 23 b).

> In a class of 50 PhD students, what are the chances of two people having exactly the same birthday:
> a) 3 in 100 or b) 97 in 100?
>
> And in a class of just 23 students:
> a) 1 in 100 or b) 50 in 100?

6.4 What kinds of questions can I ask my audience at the beginning of my presentation? (cont.)

For Q2 and Q3, you don't need a slide, but could simply give them alternatives: e.g. 33 hours, 33 days, 33 months or 33 years (33 years is the approximate answer). For Q3 you could say *which is the most common form of cancer: x or y* (two choices), *x, y or z* (three choices) More than three choices means that the audience will take too much time to think of the answer. For your question to have the most effect, you want the process of giving and answering the question to be a maximum of say 10 seconds.

b) Don't ask questions that are very 'big'. Q4 is a huge topic, but it would work if you simply said *Why do people believe in conspiracy theories?* paused for a second and then said *Well, I am going to tell you one reason that is going to change the way you think about conspiracy theorists*. In this case you are not actually asking your audience to think about the question because you answer the question almost immediately. However, you have gained their attention as they will want to hear whether your *reason* really is new and is different from theirs.

c) Don't make the audience feel stupid (Q5). Many of your audience will certainly know the answer to the question and may be wondering why you are asking them. Others will not know, and may feel ignorant for not knowing.

d) Don't wait for the audience to answer the question, unless it involves simply getting them to put their hand up (Q6).

e) Don't ask them something that may take them a long time to think of an answer (Q7) – two reasons would be enough - or which they might object to (Q7 might irritate big meat-eaters)

6.5 How should I talk about statistics as a way to introduce my research?

1. When you present, what statistics could you use to underline the importance of your research? (If you don't have any statistics, then try to find some).
2. Show your statistics to friends and family. Ask them which ones they find the most interesting. Consider using these statistics in your presentations as a way of introducing your topic and getting audience attention.

Below are statistics from the second slide of a presentation on hand prostheses, i.e. an artificial hand for someone who has had their hand amputated. The presenter's idea is to give some statistics that highlight the need for his research.

- More than one million annual limb amputations globally.
- Around 0.5% of the world's population is an amputee.
- High impact on quality of life and inability to work.
- Around 30% of people with limb loss experience depression and/or anxiety.
- High cost for the public healthcare.

The presenter thus provides the audience with a lot of interesting information. Such information gains the audience's attention and thus makes it more likely that they will pay attention to the rest of the presentation. It also makes the presentation MEMORABLE. This is a key quality of any presentation – you want what you say to be remembered, you also want the audience to remember you. If they remember you they are more likely to

- read your paper, i.e. the paper that relates to the research you presented in your presentation
- contact you – see 10.4

6.5 How should I talk about statistics as a way to introduce my research? (cont.)

The five statistics about prostheses are very interesting. But what statistic is missing? What other statistic might the audience really be interested in knowing?

The prostheses presenter gave the audience memorable info. But he did not explain WHY there are so many amputees. This is clearly a question that many members of the audience will be asking themselves.

What do you think are the main reasons why people lose their limbs?

- industrial accidents
- car and motorbike accidents
- medical conditions

The answer is on the last page of this chapter.

Did you get the answer correct? If you did, then you will be pleased with yourself and this positive emotion will also make you feel positive about the presenter. If you thought it was the result of some kind of accident then you might be surprised to hear it is due medical disorders. This sense of surprise will also leave you with a positive emotion which will directly or indirectly make you feel positive about the presenter.

Audiences enjoy both the feeling of knowing the answer and also of not knowing the answer – providing that they are not made to feel stupid for not knowing.

Instead of just giving your audience a list of statistics, you can gain more attention by getting them to think of the answers before you tell them. They will then be motivated to listen to your answers.

Giving your audience statistics is a great way of beginning a presentation. But you have to know in advance WHAT statistics your audience are most likely to be interested in.

So find lots of statistics, show them to family and friends, and pick the ones that they find the most interesting. Also, get them to ask you questions about your research, and then find statistics that you can use to answer their questions.

For more on statistics see 8.6.

For more on how to use bullet points see 8.5.

6.6 How can I begin by relating my research to my country?

1. Is your country:
   a) well known to the rest of the world?
   b) well known but often misunderstood due to the stereotypes that people have about it?
   c) big, but not very well known by people from other continents?
   d) relatively small and unknown?
2. In what ways does your research relate to the country where you come from? Think hard about this even if you are convinced there is no connection.

If you are giving a presentation and you are of a different nationality from the majority of the audience, use your native country as way to start your presentation. This works particularly well if you are from a country that most of the audience know:

- very LITTLE about
- or know a LOT about and you tell them something that they did NOT know about your country, perhaps something counterintuitive or counter-stereotypical

6.6　How can I begin by relating my research to my country? (cont.)

The slide below is the second slide by a researcher from Myanmar. He is talking about the cultivation of maize (also known as *corn*) in his country.

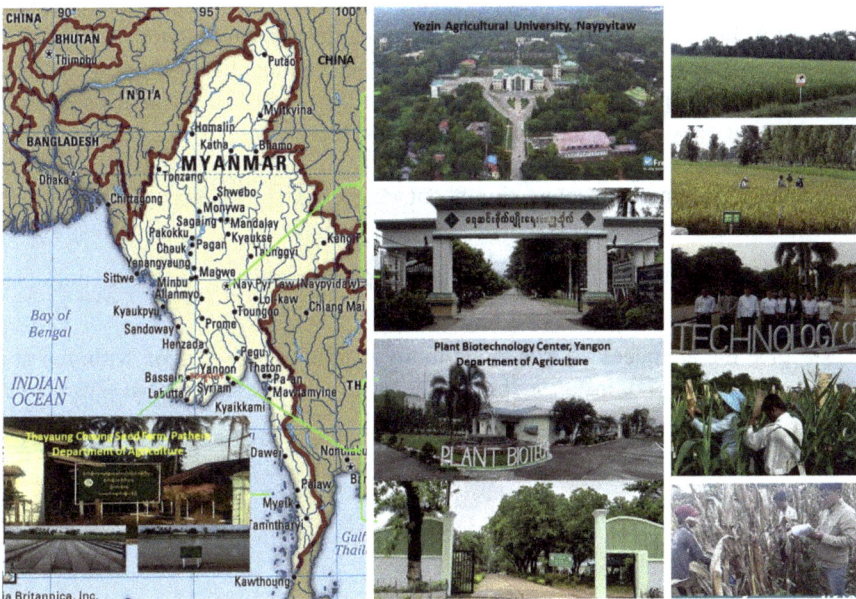

His idea to put a map of Myanmar is a good one, since many people in the audience may not be sure where exactly the country is located.

The photos also create interest for the audience as they show the institutes where he works and also the kind of vegetation typical of that part of Myanmar.

However, the slide could be improved by:

- separating it into several slides – there are 11 photographs, which means none of the photos is sufficiently big for the audience to appreciate, and having so many images is distracting – where is the audience supposed to focus?

- having a larger scale map, or possibly two maps – a large scale map, and then an indent with the smaller-scale map. A large-scale map (i.e. the whole of Asia) will give a Western audience a much clearer idea of the location, and the smaller scale map will give an indication of the size of Myanmar relative to some of its neighbors (Bangladesh, Bhutan)

6.6 How can I begin by relating my research to my country? (cont.)

One of the great things about being in the world of academia is that you have opportunities to meet people from different countries. In order to network well in academia, a key quality is being curious about other nationalities and countries. This curiosity will help you make new friends in other countries. These friends could provide you opportunities to spend periods conducting research outside your own country.

So if there is something interesting about your country that your audience don't know, tell them about it. This will

- make you memorable to the audience, particularly if you are the only presenter from that country
- give the attendees an easy opportunity to start a conversation with you at a social event. For instance, they might say to you: *So, you're from Myanmar ...*

Clearly, you may actually want to deliberately <u>avoid</u> saying where you are from because of the current political situation there, which you may wish to avoid talking about at social events.

6.7 My research area is very complex. How can I begin in a way that is not too academic and formal?

1. How complex is your research area?
2. Is it possible to explain your research area using non-complex terms? If not, why not?
3. How would you explain your research area to a non-academic, for example, to an intelligent teenager?
4. How important is it to give a 'serious' academic presentation, rather than <u>also</u> trying to entertain your audience?

Most researchers take themselves and their research very seriously. They are right to do so. However, your presentation can be both accessible and serious ... and entertaining. You will not be compromising your research if you begin your presentation in an informal way. 99% of the audience will <u>not</u> feel that you are not professional.

6.7 My research area is very complex. How can I begin in a way that is not too academic and formal? (cont.)

Below is a slide from a presentation on 'dark matter', one of the most complex areas of physics and science in general. Note how the presenter, a physicist, begins by using a series of simple phrases that will not make the audience feel stupid or ignorant.

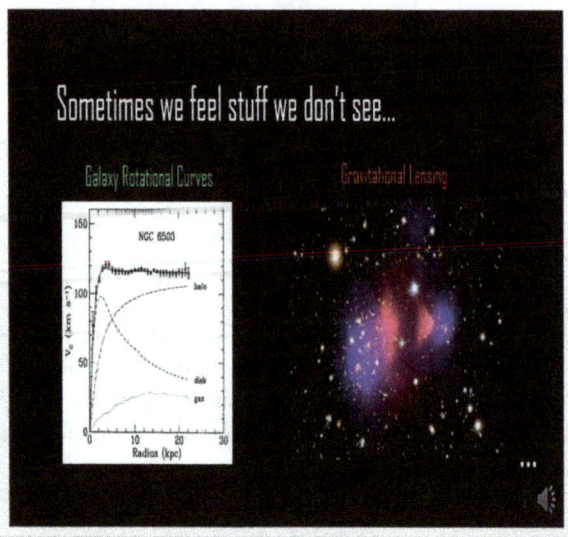

Sometimes we feel stuff we do not see. As we know, there's much more stuff out there in the universe that exerts gravity on us than we actually see. This stuff is what we call dark matter. Over the years indirect evidence for this dark matter has piled up. Dark matter flattens out galaxy rotation curves. It bends light making galaxies look

Clearly, the above slide and speech work best if the conference <u>is not</u> specifically on dark matter. If the conference <u>is</u> on dark matter, then the presenter could begin in one of the ways suggested in 6.3, 6.4 and 6.5. If you are talking to an audience of experts, then a good way to start is to give them some new or counterintuitive information about the study area that you are all working on.

In any case, nothing is too complex that it cannot be explained. As the physicist Ernest Rutherford said (in a non-PC way!) over a hundred years ago: *An alleged scientific discovery has no merit unless it can be explained to a barmaid.* Paraphrasing Rutherford's quotation, Albert Einstein said: *If you can't explain it simply, you don't understand it well enough.*

6.8 My presentation is not for a conference. How should I introduce myself?

Presentations are not just for conferences. You may have to do a presentation when you start a new project with a new team or defend your thesis in front of a board of examiners. You often need to introduce both yourself (your background) and your research.

Which do you prefer?

i) points introduced one by one via an animation.

- MD, Degree at University of Pisa (110/110 *cum laude*)

- MD, Degree at University of Pisa (110/110 *cum laude*)
- MCGEL laboratory and OB/GYN Department 2021-present

- MD, Degree at University of Pisa (110/110 *cum laude*)
- MCGEL laboratory and OB/GYN Department 2021-present
- Erasmus Traineeship in Valencia, September-October 2020

6.8 My presentation is not for a conference. How should I introduce myself? (cont.)

ii) or all at once.

- MD, Degree at University of Pisa (110/110 *cum laude*)
- MCGEL laboratory and OB/GYN Department 2021-present
- Erasmus Traineeship in Valencia, September-October 2020

Cellular and Molecular Biology in the field of gynecological endocrinology
Thesis: Modificazioni metaboliche ed infiammatorie durante la transizione menopausale

Minimally-invasive gynecological surgery

Robotic surgery for pelvic floor dysfunctions

Tranvaginal reconstructive techniques for pelvic organ prolapse

What are the advantages of the two techniques? a) for the presenter b) for the audience?

The problem with introducing your qualifications one by one using an animation is that the first thing that the audience see is one line of text in an otherwise empty slide. From a visual point of view this does not look great. Then as more bullets are added the audience may wonder when the slide will be complete. This kind of animation is not great to watch. Moreover, it forces you to:

- comment on each qualification (although you will probably end up just repeating what you have written on your slide)
- look behind you at the screen (at a live, not virtual, conference) to check which point you are up to

On the other hand, if you introduce everything all at once. You can simply say: *So this is my academic background, and by the way that's Ischia in the background of my photo, which is where I come from. It's an island off the coast of Naples in Italy.*

You can stop talking and give the audience three seconds to absorb the information and then just comment on one or maximum two of the points: *My time at the MCGEL lab was really great because ....*

6.8 My presentation is not for a conference. How should I introduce myself? (cont.)

Introducing bullet points one-by-one is really only useful when you are showing your audience a process or procedure. In this case it may be important to explain each step at a time rather than showing the entire process at once.

6.9 What doesn't the audience need / want to hear in my first 30 seconds?

What effect does the following slide have on you, particularly the words 'Climate Change'?

Many people have read and heard so much about 'climate change' that they may even stop reading or listening when you mention those two words.

You need to be aware of what your audience does and does not want to hear.

Of course, we MUST speak about climate change. But don't talk about it in general terms, quickly get to the specifics of how your research is designed to combat climate change.

An example of an original way to talk about how your research is combatting climate change

Let's look at how, Eva, a Spanish researcher, talked about climate change. Note: She was doing her presentation in Italy (hence the photo of Venice in her second slide).

6.9 What doesn't the audience need / want to hear in my first 30 seconds? (cont.)

Her research is about how climate change has increased the number of floods around the world, and how this has impacted on how certain crops are able to germinate under water. Rice has developed a kind of snorkel in order to get the oxygen it needs. Eva, however, is investigating barley. Barley is unable to germinate under submergence. However, barley can tolerate short periods of submergence, after which it is still able to germinate. Eva provides a possible genetic explanation of this phenomenon.

SLIDE 1

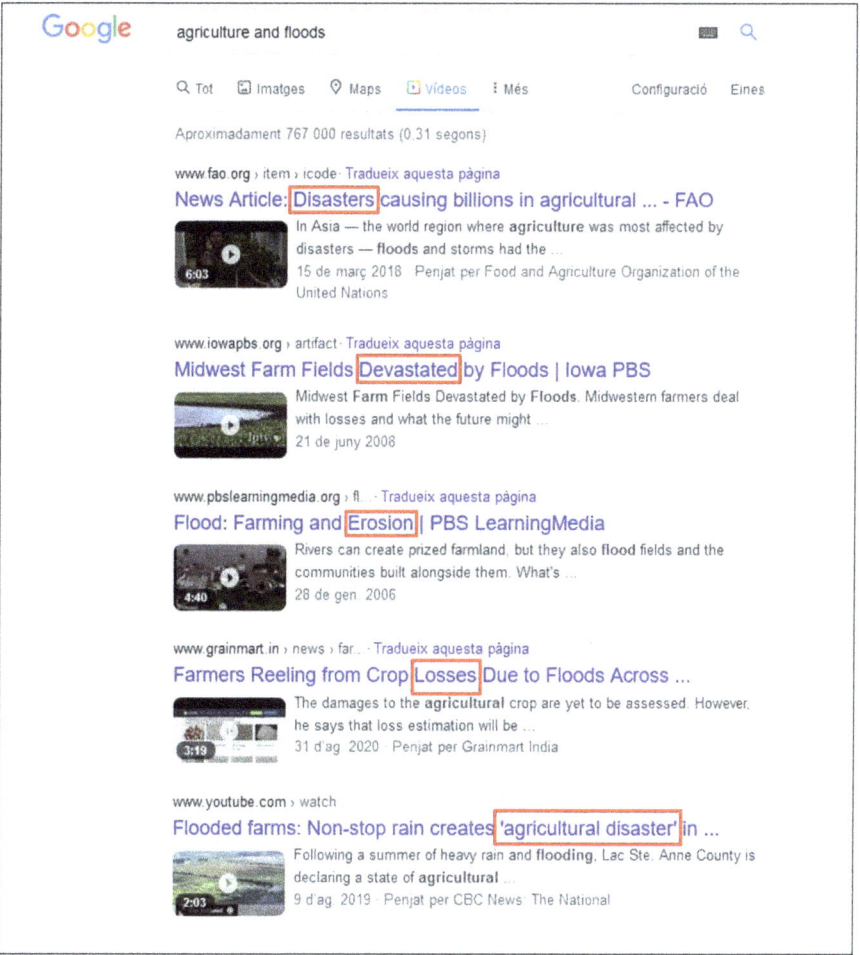

6.9 What doesn't the audience need / want to hear in my first 30 seconds? (cont.)

This is what she said:

I really did not know how to start this presentation. I work in plant responses to flooding and I did not know how to help you understand why my topic is worth studying. Thus, I did what people normally do when they do not know something: Google it. And then, I analysed which types of words were related. I looked for 'Agriculture and floods', and all the words that appear were negative: *disasters, devastated, erosion...* I thought: *this has to mean something.*

ANALYSIS OF EVA'S SCRIPT FOR FIRST SLIDE

Eva's introduction is captivating, unusual, clever and memorable. Yet she uses a classic presentation technique: She tells the audience a story. In this case it is the story of the mental process she went through while preparing her presentation. And it is a story that the audience can totally relate to – using Google when you need an answer. But the answer she got was not what she was expecting, yet totally confirmed the importance of her research.

SLIDE 2

Below is her second slide.

6.9 What doesn't the audience need / want to hear in my first 30 seconds? (cont.)

This is what she said:

This is my hometown, Valencia, one year ago. But this is also happening here in Italy. Here is Venice two years ago. This is not only important because Google says it so, or because it affects our countries. It is important because the FAO estimates that from 2006 to 2016, almost 60% of all agriculture losses were caused by flooding. So, this is a real problem that it is worth studying because it is affecting the food security of the whole world. As you can imagine, floods produce soil erosion and reduce oxygen availability. And this has dramatic consequence in the agricultural yields. However, there are some exceptions ...

ANALYSIS OF SCRIPT FOR SECOND SLIDE

Eva continues with a narrative style. She talks about herself (Valencia). In fact, talking about yourself is a great strategy for the audience to understand how where you come from is connected to the research you are doing. She also talks about the audience: the presentation was given in Italy, so the comment about Venice is clearly designed to get the audience involved.

She also continues with the Google references thus connecting back to the previous slide.

She then gives some FAO statistics that support what she is saying and give her credibility.

SLIDE 3

Her third slide then explained how rice and barley deal with periods under water. This is what she said:

Rice germinates under submergence. Rice seeds are able to elongate their coleoptile and also to degrade starchy reserves. But rice is an exception. Barley seeds cannot germinate under submergence. Barley hates flooding. However, I saw in the literature that some barley varieties can tolerate short periods of submergence, but the genetic basis of this response is still unknown. And that is what I am working on. In our research group we are doing a genome-wide association study to analyse the genetic response of the tolerant barley accessions to flooding.

6.9 What doesn't the audience need / want to hear in my first 30 seconds? (cont.)

ANALYSIS OF SCRIPT FOR THIRD SLIDE

Note how her script is very simple. Short sentences. Repetition of key words. Clear comparison of rice and barley. By the end of this third slide the audience are clear:

- what the problem is
- how serious the problem is
- how one plant, rice, deals with the problem, and how another plant, barley, cannot deal with the problem
- the solution to the barley problem

Eva has presented all this information in a way that immediately captures the audience's attention, and then keeps this attention through simple slides with simple explanations.

6.10 How important is my English at the beginning of my presentation?

There are two key aspects regarding your use of English at a conference:

- your accent, pronunciation, and intonation
- your grammar and vocabulary

It is difficult for you to control your accent. In any case, if you speak slowly and articulate each word clearly, your accent is unlikely to have a negative impact on the audience.

Your pronunciation is important, and is certainly something you can control – you only need to learn the correct pronunciation of the words that you will use during your presentation (see 4.2).

Your intonation, too, is important. The audience will lose concentration if they hear a monotone voice.

Even if you make mistakes with your grammar and vocabulary, the audience will usually still understand you. But the impression you may give is that you didn't take the time to the learn the English you needed for this presentation. Given that the transcript of 10-minute presentation only occupies about two A4 size sheets, there is really no excuse not to have good grammar and the correct vocabulary.

To learn more about writing a script and your pronunciation, see Chapters 3 and 4.

If you didn't take the time to ensure that your pronunciation and grammar are correct, this <u>could</u> indicate to the audience that you don't take your research seriously enough to want to give a good presentation. The result is that some people in the audience may decide that you are not very credible.

What you say at the beginning of your presentation will determine the first impression that the audience has.

You want to make a good first impression as this will condition how the audience listen to the rest of your presentation. If you begin well and speak in fairly accurate English and your slides do not contain English errors, then you are increasing your chances of attracting and retaining your audience's attention.

6.9 How important is my English at the beginning of my presentation? (cont.)

Clearly, the audience's first impression does not only depend on your English. Your audience is not made up of English teachers! What is more important is WHAT you say (i.e. the content), rather than just HOW you say it. Nevertheless, HOW you say something can vastly improve what you say or, on the contrary, vastly undermine what you say.

> **Answer to exercises in 6.5**
>
> In the USA the main causes of amputations are vascular disease (54%), trauma (45%) and cancer (less than 2%). Vascular diseases include diabetes and peripheral arterial disease.

Chapter 7
Agenda

7.1 Do I need an agenda?

1. What is an agenda?
2. Do you use an agenda in your presentations? Why (not)?
3. Is an agenda essential? What happens if there is no agenda?
4. Why is the agenda slide below probably of little use to the audience?

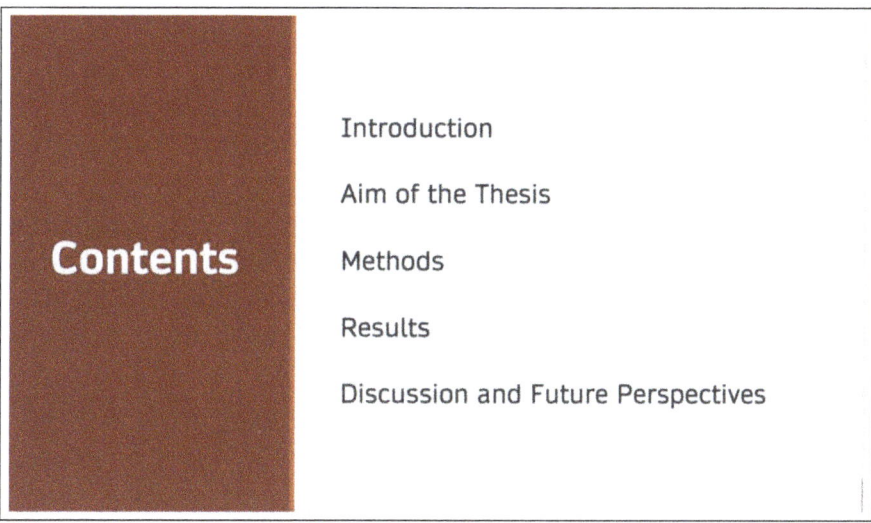

7.1 Do I need an agenda? (cont.)

The agenda above tells the audience what they already know. It is the typical structure of a presentation. So an agenda of this sort is of little help either to the audience or the presenter.

Look at this typical script to accompany the agenda slide above. It gives no concrete information, but unfortunately is very common in academic presentations.

Here we have a brief summary of the contents of this presentation. I divided it into some sections, a brief introduction in which I'll analyze the background we can find in scientific literature and that supports the aim of my thesis. Then, we'll find the main methods I applied to obtain of course the results that I am going to tell you. And, after that, I'll spend some time discussing these results and underlining my planned experiments on this topic.

An agenda reassures the audience that there is a structure to your presentation, which they will be able to follow. Having a clear structure means that the audience know at what point they are in each slide. However, the agenda slide above fails to do this.

Some presenters have a dedicated agenda slide. Others just explain their agenda without listing the various points on a specific slide.

If you do not have an agenda, the audience might not be clear how your presentation will develop and may become frustrated when it does not develop in the way that they were expecting.

I suggest that you do tell your audience how your presentation is structured. You can do this verbally, without necessarily having a dedicated slide.

The rest of this chapter explains what to include in an agenda slide if you have decided that such a slide is necessary or will be expected by your audience.

7.2 What should I call my agenda? What heading should I use?

Below are four different headings for an agenda slide. How useful are they?

Agenda

Outline

Coverage

What I am going to talk about

Microsoft PowerPoint and many other presentation software applications encourage you to have a heading for each slide. This heading is also in a much bigger font size than the rest of the slide. The eyes of the audience are thus attracted towards these big headings. The headings given above (Agenda, Abstract etc.) do not deserve the importance of a big font. They add provide no useful information for the audience.

So, consider <u>not</u> having a heading in your agenda slide.

7.3 How should I present and explain my agenda?

Below are two agendas for the same presentation entitled: *Why don't you use Google Translate? Five reasons why non-native English-speaking academics should use GT to translate their papers rather than writing them directly in English.* In these two agendas, GT stands for Google Translate, and TQA stands for Translation Quality Assessment.

Decide which agenda is best and why?

> Is GT more accurate than you?
>
> Why so few PhD students use GT.
>
> How we proved you should use it.
>
> What would change if you did use it.
>
> Help our team to help you.

> - INTRO: Proximity of measurement results to true value in PhD translation performance vs GT
> - LIT. REVIEW: Scarcity of PhD automatic translation usage
> - METHODOLOGY AND VALIDATION OF RESULTS – semantic adequacy
> - DISCUSSION AND CONCLUSIONS: Implications of TQAs and extended use of GT

The choice is subjective and may depend on the type of conference (and the expectations of the audience).

However, if your aim is for your audience to have a clear picture of your research, of how it relates to them personally, and to enlist their support for your project, then certainly the first is best. It is also quick to read and assimilate.

7.3 How should I present and explain my agenda? (cont.)

The second 'looks' very academic and serious, but why make your audience work hard in trying to understand what is written? Also the impression that the audience might get from the second agenda is that the presentation is going to be very technical. The use of Intro, Lit. Review etc. is not strictly necessary because it simply follows a standard presentation structure that the audience will be expecting.

Look at this agenda again.

> Is GT more accurate than you?
>
> Why so few PhD students use GT.
>
> How we proved you should use it.
>
> What would change if you did use it.
>
> Help our team to help you.

The scripts below show two alternatives of what a presenter could say while showing the agenda slide above. Which one would the audience be able to follow the best? Why? What is the problem with the other one?

ALTERNATIVE 1

So this my agenda. First I'll show you that Google Translate is 20% more accurate than you are. If you are a typical student, you probably don't use GT because you've seen (or read on the net) that it makes some very big mistakes. Or maybe you used at school and don't know how much it has improved since then. How did we prove that it is more accurate? By testing 10000 students. In 95% of cases, Google was more accurate. So, what would change if you used it? I will show you how, for a typical 20-page research paper, GT will save you around 20 hours … AND be more accurate. By the end of the presentation, I hope you will be interested in helping our team and I will give you details on how to do this.

ALTERNATIVE 2

So this my agenda. We tested over 10000 PhD students and revealed that Google Translate is at least 20% more accurate than them. I will show many examples of translations done by PhD students and their professors which highlight that although Google makes mistakes, they tend to be quite big mistakes that are easy to spot, whereas students and profs are unable to spot the mistakes that they themselves make. It would be great if you could take part in our survey.

7.3 How should I present and explain my agenda? (cont.)

In the second version there is no match between what the presenter says and what the agenda slide. This is a very common mistake, and not just in agenda slides. It is confusing for the audience if what you are saying does not refer to what is on the slide.

Instead, the first version covers all the points in the agenda in the same order as they appear in the slide. This makes it easier for the audience to follow. The presenter also repeats some of the words from the agenda (*How did we prove that it is more accurate? So, what would change if you used it?*) – again this makes the agenda very easy to follow. This agenda is like a good abstract for a paper: it tells you the entire contents of the presentation. It also makes you interested to listen because it highlights the benefits of listening.

7.4 When explaining my agenda, should I also mention what I will NOT be covering?

Yes. For three reasons:

1. If your title indicates a wide area of research, it is helpful for the audience to know which aspects you will NOT be talking about. They will then understand where the focus will be and what they can expect.

2. In some areas of research there are aspects that most of the audience will already know. If you tell your audience that you will NOT be covering these well-known areas, then they will be reassured that they will be learning something new from you.

3. Finally, there are some topics that may invoke a negative feeling for the audience. If you tell them that you will NOT cover these areas, they may find this reassuring.

Let me give an example of Point 2 (an example of Point 3 is given at the end of this section). During the courses I give to PhD students on writing and presentation skills, I make it clear that I will NOT be focusing on grammar and vocabulary. This is important because most students associate an English course precisely with grammar and vocabulary, so they may have been expecting grammar and vocabulary to be an integral part of my course. Other students may be very glad to hear that there will be no grammar and vocabulary, and that they will be learning something different. In fact, the courses are all about communication strategies of the kind you are reading here in this chapter.

So when I give my agenda, first I tell students what I will NOT be covering and then what I WILL be covering – but I could also do it the other way round.

The order you choose (*not covering + covering*, or *covering + not covering*) will depend on your topic or on what you want to emphasize.

Now let's look at Point 3 (negative feelings).

Imagine you are going to talk about climate change, specifically how you can improve the environment through organic chemistry. Which of the following do you think the audience will want to hear:

1. How climate change is getting worse.

2. How governments are doing very little to combat climate change.

7.4 When explaining my agenda, should I also mention what I will NOT be covering? (cont.)

3. New statistics on new catastrophic events related to climate change.
4. What the audience can do themselves in their daily life to combat climate change.
5. What Greta Thunberg, the Swedish environmental activist, is currently doing to challenge world leaders.

Many audiences have overdosed (i.e. heard too much) on climate change (6.9). Although they know that the environment is crucial to the future of the planet, the audience don't necessarily want to be reminded about this at a conference.

Below is the second slide of a presentation given by an organic chemist.

This is what the chemist said:

> I study green chemistry. I want to tell you about a new way to reduce the impact of industrial processes and help sustain the environment. **But don't worry, I am not going to** be giving you lots of worrying statistics on climate change. Instead I am going to talk about catalysts and ligands, and ....

The image and the speech are designed to create a relaxed atmosphere and also to tell the audience that they are not going to have to listen to yet another presentation on the dangers of climate change. Instead they are going to hear about a <u>new</u> solution.

7.5 Is it a good idea to start by giving the audience the 'big picture'?

Many academic presentations begin with a title slide in which the presenter simply announces the topic of their research and then begins talking about this topic, typically about the aims of the project.

This approach is not effective because:

- it is what most presenters do. It is thus unlikely to attract the attention of the audience – they've seen it all before
- it doesn't give the audience time to get used to your voice – remember that your accent may not be familiar to the audience so they need time to adjust to it
- audiences need a few moments to stop thinking about the previous presentation (or the phone call they have just made, or the conversation during the lunch break) and to switch to focusing on you

Instead a good approach is to use the first minute to give the big picture (see 6.1). This means giving an overall perspective on the problem you are trying to solve. You do not go into the details at this point.

So you first outline the problem in a reasonably non-technical way. You can do this via images, statistics (e.g. through an interesting graph) or simply by talking with no accompanying slide.

The audience will thus get an idea of the context and background. You can then tell them

1. why this problem needs solving
2. what will happen if it is NOT solved
3. how your research aims to solve this problem
4. what you are doing to solve the problem, and at what stage you are at with this solution

By first explaining the big picture you enable the audience to then understand why you are doing your research. The audience will thus be more motivated to hear the solution.

Without the big picture, the audience might get quickly lost in your description of a solution to a problem that they don't really understand – i.e. if they don't understand the problem, then the solution will make little sense.

7.6 When explaining my agenda, how can I encourage the audience to listen carefully and possibly to collaborate with me in the future?

First let's remember what the main aim of a presentation is (1.7). Which TWO of the following are the most important aims?

1. Disseminate your research and encourage the audience to read your paper. The community will then know what you are doing.
2. Make yourself known / Gain visibility in your field so that you will be invited to other conferences.
3. Make contacts with people who can help you with your research.
4. Improve you job possibilities + career.
5. Be memorable so that audience will want to contact you and possibly collaborate with you.
6. Give the impression of being an approachable person who would be easy to talk with and work with.

They are all important. However, 1-4 strictly depend on 5 and 6. If your presentation is not memorable then your research is unlikely to be disseminated, you will be forgotten: so no visibility. No one will make contact with you, and so you career will not advance.

Instead if you are memorable and approachable (i.e. you seem to be the kind of person who it would be easy to get along / talk with), people will want to contact you and collaborate with you. As a consequence you may have a greater chance of getting funds and continuing your work.

This means your entire presentation should be designed to get the audience interested in collaborating with you.

Below is the script from the presenter on green chemistry. Can you identify which sentences are designed to encourage the audience to think about a possible collaboration?

7.6 When explaining my agenda, how can I encourage the audience to listen carefully and possibly to collaborate with me in the future? (cont.)

I study green chemistry. I want to tell you about a new way to reduce the impact of industrial processes and help sustain the environment. But don't worry, I am not going to be giving you lots of worrying statistics on climate change. Instead I am going to talk about catalysts and ligands, and how we can replace toxic metals with ones that are safe and also cheap and easy to find. Then I'll show you I plan to create my green catalysts. And finally, I'll explain how I think they could be applied to do x, y and z. I haven't found the perfect solution yet. So while you're listening, if any ideas come to you, then please let me know. I will give you my email at the end. *moves to next slide.* So here is the problem. At the moment we use a lot of toxic metals – the ones you can see in the slide ...

The key phrases are:

1. I haven't found the perfect solution yet.

2. So while you're listening, if any ideas come to you, then please let me know.

3. I will give you my email at the end.

4. But don't worry, I am not going to be giving you lots of worrying statistics on climate change.

Sentence 1 tells the audience that the presenter's work is still ongoing. In fact, it tells the audience that this researcher actually has a problem i.e. no solution at the moment. It is part of human nature to want to help other people (see Chapter 10). So this sentence cleverly encourages the audience to think of possible solutions while they are watching the presentation (Sentence 2). This has an additional advantage: the audience will listen with more attention.

Sentence 3 will make the audience be attentive during the presenter's last slide as they will (hopefully) want the presenter's contact details. The sentence also puts the idea into the audience's head that they will want to contact the presenter.

Sentence 4 comes from earlier in the speech. It is designed to highlight that the presenter is thinking about the audience – he/she cares about them and knows they don't want to hear another horror story. This sentence further emphasizes that the presenter is an empathetic person, with a sense of humor, and who is likely to be easy to approach and talk with.

7.7 What tenses in English do I need when outlining my agenda to the audience?

Below is an extract from an English language textbook on the tenses required in English (present, future) when outlining an agenda.

- How useful is it?
- How much of what it says do you think you need to learn?

> There is a wide variety of tenses you can use when outlining your agenda. Most presenters tend to mix them to create variety. There is practically no difference in meaning.
>
> **Present simple**
>
> Used to introduce the agenda – it is more formal than the present continuous.
>
> *This is what I plan to do today.*
>
> Not used when describing the list of items you intend to cover.
>
> *First, I look at x, then I move on to y. = First I will look at x, then I will move on to y.*
>
> **Present continuous**
>
> Used to introduce the agenda – it is more informal than the simple present.
>
> *This is what I am planning to do today.*
>
> Not used when describing the list of items you intend to cover.
>
> *First, I am looking at x, = First I will look at x,*
>
> **Will (future simple) and Going to**
>
> Using only *will* is not heavy to listen to, but gives a very formal tone to your presentation.
>
> *I will begin with an introduction to ... Then I will move on to ... After that I will deal with ... And I will conclude with ...*

7.7 What tenses in English do I need when outlining my agenda to the audience? (cont.)

The problem with the examples above is that they encourage you to use phrases that the audience have heard so many times before and thus may not pay attention to them. If they don't pay attention at the beginning of your presentation, you risk losing their attention completely.

So, you don't <u>necessarily</u> need the typical phrases given above.

Listen to how presenters on ted.com begin their presentations. Do they use any of the phrases given in the English language textbook? Probably not.

Make a pencil draft of your agenda slide. Think about:

- A heading – do you need one? If so, what heading?
- Images – do you need them? If so, what images?
- Text – do you need text? If so, keep it as short as possible.

Then 'add notes' about what you would say.

7.7 What tenses in English do I need when outlining my agenda to the audience? (cont.)

7.1-7.4, *English for Presentations at International Conferences*

Chapter 8
Explaining technical slides

8.1 Why do I need to keep my slides simple?

Below is the second slide of a presentation on pancreatic cancer given by a medical student.

Imagine that you too are a medical student. Would you know where to focus your eyes first? Do you think all your colleagues would focus on the same place?

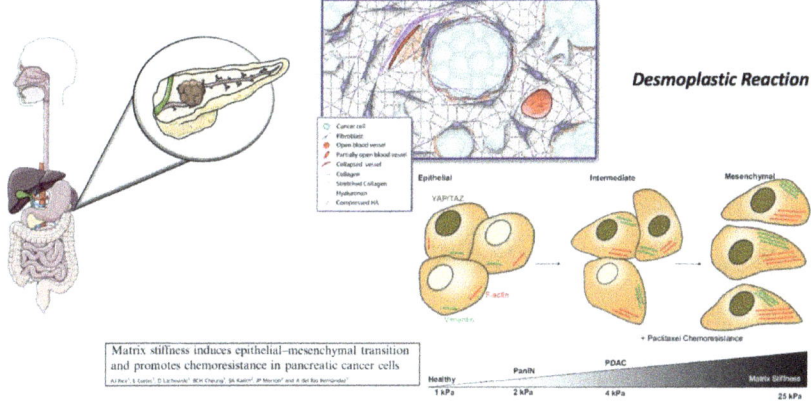

8.1 Why do I need to keep my slides simple? (cont.)

In the slide, there are four areas where the audience might focus their attention: top left (human body), top right (desmplastic reaction – it is not clear whether this refers to the image to the left, or the image below), bottom left (text), bottom right (image + graph). As a presenter, you cannot be sure where your audience will look first. The problem is that if they are looking at one thing and you are describing another, then they will not be following your presentation as you had planned.

If you have a series of images that describe a process, then you could number the images. Or you could use an animation to focus on one image at a time, or one part of the slide at a time.

However, the simplest solution is to break up the slide into more slides. So in this case you could have 3-4 slides. The time it takes you to explain these 3-4 slides will not be longer than it would take to explain the one original slide. And by having more slides, you can be sure that your audience will be focusing on what you want them to focus on.

Follow the KISS principle: Keep It Short and Simple.

8.2 I need my audience to see a lot of detail. What can I do?

Imagine you are at a conference. You have already seen five presentations today. Which type of presentation would you like to see now: i) ones full of slides like this one?

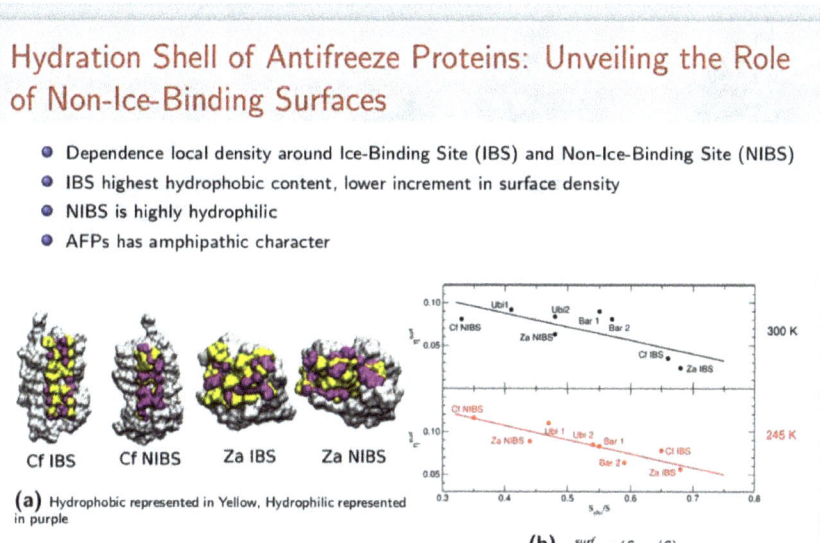

Zanetti-Polzi, L., **Biswas, A. D.**, Del Galdo, S., Barone, V., & Daidone, I. (2019). Hydration Shell of Antifreeze Proteins: Unveiling the Role of Non-Ice-Binding Surfaces. The Journal of Physical Chemistry B, 123(30), 6474-6480.

8.2 I need my audience to see a lot of detail. What can I do? (cont.)

or ii) slides like this one?

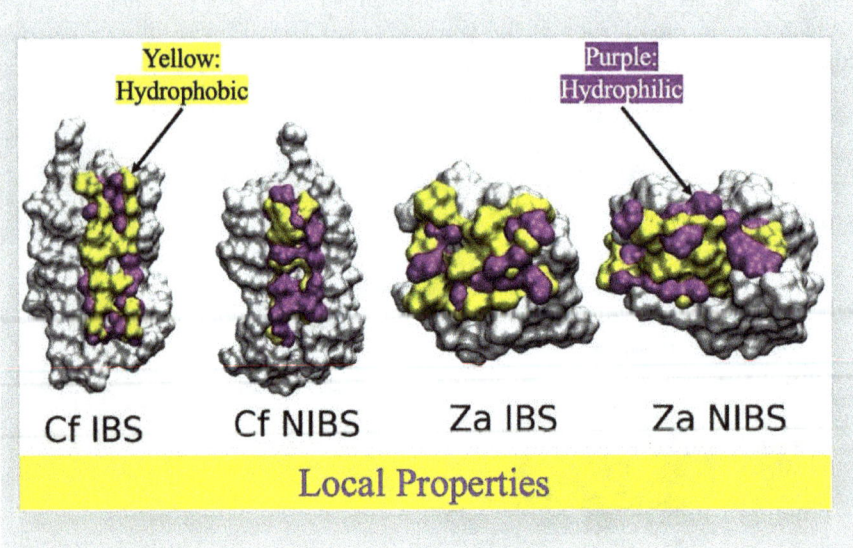

What are the pros and cons of the two types of slides?

The underlying philosophy of this book is this: The main aim of your presentation is NOT to provide a mass of information to your audience.

Your main aim is to get the audience sufficiently interested that they will want to: i) read your paper, ii) collaborate with you, iii) cite your wok in their own work.

Consequently, you need to make the audience's job easy. Also, a lot depends on when during the conference day your presentation is. If it is the first presentation of the day, then you can expect your audience to have a high degree of mental energy. But if it is in the afternoon, their energy levels will be low, and they will be much happier to see the simpler slides rather than the complex ones.

8.2 I need my audience to see a lot of detail. What can I do? (cont.)

Consider having TWO versions of your presentation

Version 1: minimal text, minimal graphics.

Version 2: much more text and more detailed tables, figures; same number and order of slides as in Version 1.

Use Version 1 in your real presentation to the audience. It will be easy for you to say/explain and easy for your audience to understand. Give audience access to Version 2 (e.g. upload on conference website or give viewers the url), then if they don't understand something you've said or if they miss the presentation entirely, then they can refer to this version.

Here are some example slides from the technical part of a presentation entitled: *A computational study on the hydration-shell properties of antifreeze and non-antifreeze proteins.* Don't worry if you understand nothing about the content (I don't either!), you just need to understand the benefits of the two different versions.

VERSION 1 (MINIMAL SLIDES THAT YOU SHOW THE AUDIENCE):

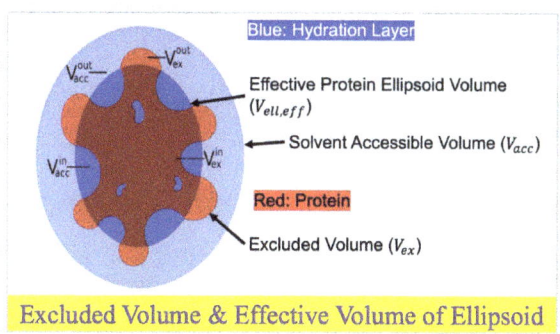

Excluded Volume & Effective Volume of Ellipsoid

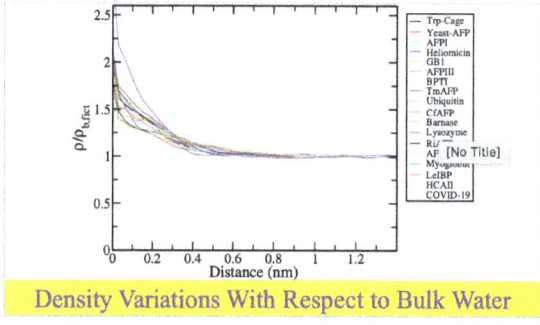

Density Variations With Respect to Bulk Water

8.2 I need my audience to see a lot of detail. What can I do? (cont.)

VERSION 2 (THE SLIDES THAT YOUR AUDIENCE CAN DOWNLOAD IF THEY WANT):

Length-scale Dependence of Protein Hydration-shell Density

- Model: $\eta = \frac{\rho_{sh}}{\rho_b} - 1$
  where:
  η = relative density increment,
  ρ_{sh} = density within the hydration shell,
  ρ_b = density within the bulk
- Protein size dependence of hydration shell density of AFPs do not differ from Non-AFPs

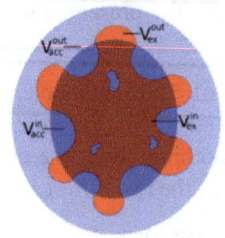

- Blue: hydration shell, V_{sh}
- Dark Blue: effective protein ellipsoid volume, $V_{ell,eff}$
- Blue: solvent-accessible volume, V_{acc}
- Red: excluded protein volume, V_{ex}
- Dark red: V_{ex}^{in}

(a) Schematic diagram showing the main parameters used in the model

Length-scale Dependence of Protein Hydration-shell Density

- Dependence of protein hydration-shell density on the size and shape of protein molecules

(b) Protein size (Residue N.), relative density increment, η

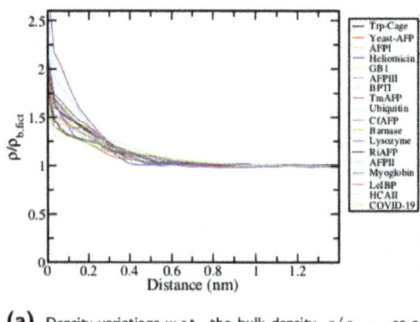

(a) Density variations w.r.t. the bulk density, $\rho/\rho_{b,fict}$ as a function of the distance from the protein ellipsoid surface for the eighteen proteins

Protein	Residue N.	$V_{ell,eff}$	$\frac{V_{shell}}{V_{ell,eff}}$	η
Trp-cage	20	4.46	5.95	0.050
Yeast-AFP	25	6.87	4.97	0.052
AFPI	37	8.06	4.86	0.046
Heliomicin	44	9.47	4.38	0.065
GB1	56	11.81	4.00	0.079
AFPIII	66	12.27	3.91	0.071
BPTI	56	12.41	3.94	0.068
TmAFP	82	12.46	4.00	0.083
Ubiquitin	75	14.40	3.70	0.090
CfAFP	121	19.65	3.37	0.088
Barnase	108	20.55	3.30	0.094
Lysozyme	129	22.64	3.19	0.099
RiAFP	143	23.26	3.26	0.089
AFPII	129	25.70	3.06	0.106
Myoglobin	154	28.63	2.99	0.111
LeIBP	241	38.73	2.73	0.123
HCAII	261	46.61	2.56	0.133
CoV-2	306	54.93	2.56	0.125

8.2 I need my audience to see a lot of detail. What can I do? (cont.)

Note how from a presenters' point of view, the Version 1 slides are much easier to manage and talk about. And from an audience's point of view, the Version 1 slides are easier to absorb quickly. The audience can thus listen to what the presenter is saying rather than trying to understand the mass of information on the slide.

The audience can download the Version 2 slides:

- <u>before</u> the presentation and then have them open on their phone/laptop to enable them to see more detail

or

- <u>after</u> the presentation to learn more about what the presenter has said

Note: Ideally, you should have the same number of slides in the two versions. The slides in Version 2 should preferably be in the same order as those in Version 1. This enables people who are interested in the details to read Version 2 while they are watching Version 1.

See also 12.5.

Open one of your own presentations. Find two of the fullest slides. See if you can produce minimal versions of these two slides. Then produce a script (see Chapter 3) for your new minimal slides.

8.3 Graphs. How should I explain them?

When you have created a graph, look at it from the audience's point of view and think about what questions they are likely to ask themselves. Make sure the graph answers those questions clearly and doesn't confuse the audience.

The slide below is the second slide, where the presenter introduces her work. Look at the graph, what do you expect the presenter to tell you when explaining the graph?

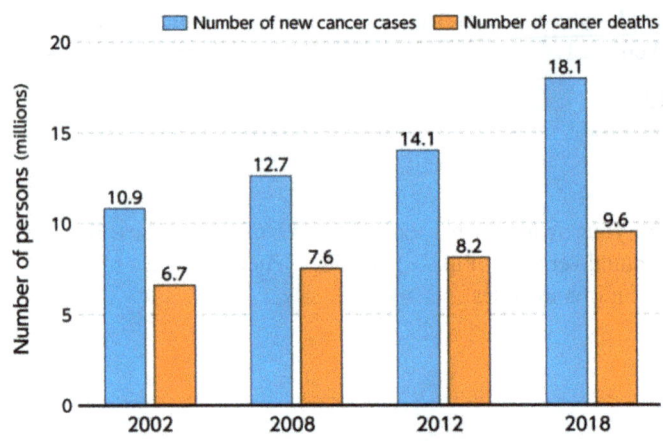

This is what the presenter said:

Do you know how many people are affected by cancer in the world? These graphs show the trend of new cancer cases and deaths in the last two decades. As you see this trend is continuously increasing. When treating cancer, it is crucial to identify tissue abnormalities for the diagnosis and management of the disease. With the correct diagnosis, we can make the right treatment. If the number of biopsies increases, the tissue samples to be analyzed in the anatomic pathology laboratory, increase as well. This is reflected in a delay in the diagnosis and in the management of the therapy that a patient needs. This is one of the reasons why the number of

8.3 Graphs. How should I explain them? (cont.)

cancer deaths is increasing over time. Indeed, if there is a delay in the diagnosis, it could be too late to save the patient affected by cancer at the advanced stages of its development.

Most audiences will look at the graph and ask themselves: *Why is the number of new cancer cases increasing?* And they will probably also ask: *And what about this year? What are the number of cases now?*

The presenter hasn't immediately answered or made reference to either of these two questions. This is because she initially focuses solely on the topic of her research. Instead she should provide the big picture (6.1) for the audience and answer the obvious question regarding this constant increase. The underlined sentence in her speech needs to be said much earlier.

It can be a good tactic to ask the audience a question (6.4). However in this case when showing the slide, it makes no sense to ask the question *Do you know how many people are affected by cancer in the world?* as the audience can immediately see the answer. In this case, a better approach would be to

- begin the presentation with a blank (i.e. completely white) slide
- ask the question
- wait for 2-3 seconds
- show the graph

In this way the audience will be more motivated to look for the answer in the graph.

The reason why the most recent date is 2018, and not the current year, is because the presenter could not find a graph with more recent data. The problem is that this looks lazy. It is also frustrating for the audience who are probably most interested in the situation today, not several years ago.

Below is an alternative speech:

The main reason why the number of cancer patients is growing is because our average life span is growing, we are living longer. In 2018 there were 18.1 million new cases, today that figure is around 20 million. Interestingly in the US the rate is actually going down for key cancers such as lung, breast and prostate.

But another key factor, which is the topic of my research, is how and when cancer is diagnosed. The earlier it is diagnosed, the better the chance of survival. My aim is to introduce an automation in the anatomic pathology laboratories so that the anatomopathologist can better diagnose the cancer.

With the correct diagnosis when we can make the right treatment.

8.3 Graphs. How should I explain them? (cont.)

This alternative speech:

- makes direct reference to the graph
- answers both the questions that the audience might have asked themselves
- talks about the big picture first before going into the details of the presenter's research topic (remember this is the second slide, i.e. the first slide after the title). Alternatively, it could be the first slide, with the title slide in second place (5.5).

8.4 Bullet points: How do I show them?

Below are three ways to present bullet points. Which solution do you think is the most effective? Why? Don't worry if you can't read the text

1) ONE BULLET POINT AT A TIME.

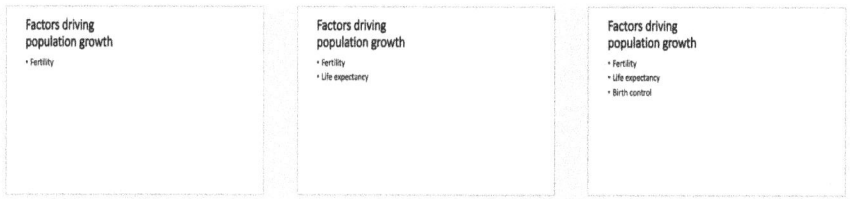

2) ALL BULLETS AT ONCE, but with the point you are talking about is highlighted (*fertility* in the first slide, life *expectancy* in the second).

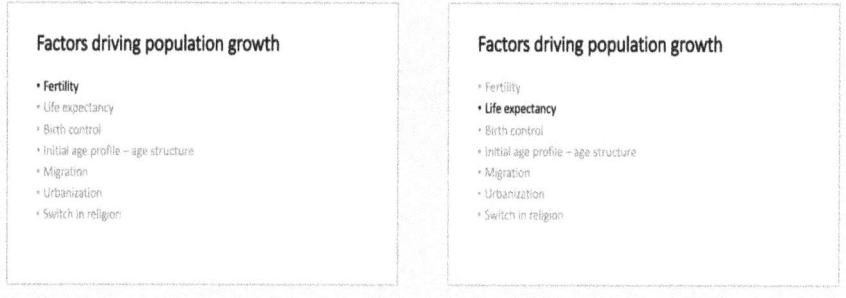

8.4 Bullet points: How do I show them? (cont.)

3) AUDIENCE SEES ALL BULLETS AT THE SAME TIME.

> **Factors driving population growth**
>
> - Fertility
> - Life expectancy
> - Birth control
> - Initial age profile – age structure
> - Migration
> - Urbanization
> - Switch in religion

🔑

1) This solution, using an 'animation' * , is very popular among presenters, but not so popular for audiences! It allows the presenter to focus on one bullet point at a time. However, for the audience the effect is different: they have no idea how many bullet points there are going to be.

If I am in the audience and I see the slide below I think: *Oh no! There are going to be a lot of points and the presenter is going to talk about every single one! I don't know if I have the mental energy to follow this. I'll just see if I have any messages on my phone.* Moreover, the slide is not very attractive with all the white space.

> Factors driving
> population growth
> - Fertility

8.4 Bullet points: How do I show them? (cont.)

2) In this solution, the audience sees all the points at once and is thus reassured that there is a limited number of points – seven in total. But as in Solution 1, the audience also knows that the presenter is going to talk about every single point – seven points. Again, this is going to require a lot of mental energy from the audience. Also, they are going to see basically the same slide seven times. Instead you want to create variety in your slides to keep you audience's attention.

3) For me, this is the best solution, and this is what you should say:

These are the main causes of population growth. [Pauses two seconds to give the audience time to read all seven points]. *I studied all seven factors, but I just want to focus on the first two now.*

In summary you i) show all the bullets, ii) let the audience absorb them without you talking, iii) talk about just one or two of them.

Your aim in your presentation is not to provide the audience with a full coverage of what you did in your research. Your aim is simply to get them interested so that they will contact you for further details or so that they will want to collaborate with you. So do NOT talk about all your bullets, just limit yourself to one or two. The result is that the audience will:

- not be bombarded with information
- appreciate the fact that you have decided what points are the most important for them to understand
- not have to look at the same slide for several minutes, and thus lose their concentration and interest

* By 'animations' I do not mean animated movies like a Disney film. Instead, I mean animations that are used to build up a diagram that shows, for example, how a piece of machinery works, or the steps in a process. In this case you add one piece of visual information at a time. Animations are useful in diagrams, but not, in my opinion to introduce pieces of text one at a time.

For more on bullets see 9.2.

8.5 Bullet points to show statistics. How can I use them effectively?

Below is the second slide of a presentation given by a PhD student in biorobotics. His research group designs prostheses, i.e. artificial body parts. In his case he designs prostheses for people who have lost a limb (an arm, a leg). I already talked about this presentation in 6.5. Here I am focusing on how to present these bullet points.

Why prostheses?

- More than one million annual limb amputations globally.
- Around 0.5% of global population are amputees.
- High impact on quality of life and inability to work.
- Around 30% of people with limb loss experience depression and/or anxiety.
- High cost for the public healthcare.

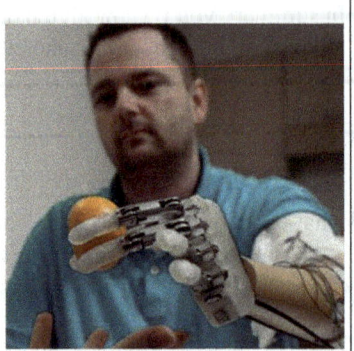

This is what he said to accompany the first two bullets:

BULLET 1 So there are one million amputations per year which corresponds to one every 30 seconds. Here in Italy there are 14,000 a year which means about 40 per day.

BULLET 2 To give you an idea of what 0.5% of the world population means: there are more amputees worldwide than there are taxi drivers.

Note that instead of just repeating what he has put in his bullets, he adds extra information. Much of this extra info is surprising and thus will:

- gain the audience's attention
- be memorable for the audience, i.e. the info will make an impact on the audience's brain which will help them remember the presentation ... and the presenter

8.5 Bullet points to show statistics. How can I use them effectively? (cont.)

A problem with the technique outlined above is that some of the audience may focus on the written text and others on what the presenter is saying.

A better solution might be to have shorter bullets, so that the audience can very quickly absorb the main point by looking at the slide, and then be able to concentrate on what the presenter is saying.

> ➢ 1,000,00+ amputations p.a.
>
> ➢ 0.5% of world population
>
> ➢ Impacts life & work
>
> ➢ 30% ⇒ depression and/or anxiety
>
> ➢ High cost for public healthcare

The bullets are:

- prompts for the presenter, i.e. they remind the presenter what to say
- incomplete short sentences: the audience can read them quickly and then really focus on what the presenter is saying because they want to hear the full meaning and explanation

8.6 Statistics. What kind of statistics do audiences like?

Knowing how to use statistics to get your audience interested involves similar decisions to those you make if you decide to ask your audience a question to gain their attention (6.4).

I am English but I live in Pisa, Italy. Below is the content from slide that I use for my courses on English for Scientific Communication (https://e4ac.com/courses). I ask my students to choose the three most interesting statistics about the Leaning Tower of Pisa.

Which three would you choose and why?

1. There are three leaning towers in Pisa
2. Designed by Bonanno Pisano
3. Construction begins in 1173 (ends 1370)
4. Galileo did his most famous experiments from the Tower
5. Weight: 14,500 tonnes
6. Inclination of 38 cm
7. Only 55.86 m high
8. 294 steps

8.6　Statistics. What kind of statistics do audiences like? (cont.)

9. It leaned 5.5 degrees in 1990
10. One million tourists per year
11. Five suicides per year
12. Over 40,000 scientific articles written about the Tower
13. Features in a Superman film

Often you have a series of statistics available in relation to your research. You don't have time to present all of them, so you need to choose which ones are the most pertinent to your study AND will also be of interest to your audience.

My students, many of whom are Italian and thus familiar with the Tower, all seem to choose 1 and 12, and one other. **1** and **12** are excellent choices because they are not what the audience is expecting, therefore they attract attention.

2-4 Statistics like these are quite dry. If you mention someone relatively obscure (Bonanno Pisano) then it might help if you mention him in association with someone that that audience will know (e.g. he was married to Leonardo da Vinci's sister) or that you say something unusual about him (e.g. he slept in the tower every night while it was being built). I have just invented these details, but the idea is to stimulate the audience's interest. In the case of 4, perhaps you could mention what the most famous experiments were.

5-10 These are all potentially interesting, but many of them can only come 'alive' if they are compared with something else. By themselves, they tell the audience very little. 5) Is 14,500 tonnes a lot or a little for a building that size? 6) Is 38 cm a big or small inclination? 7) 'Only' 55.86 m high – does that 'only' imply that the tower is not very tall? 8) Is 294 a lot of steps? 9) Why do we want to know about 1990? 10) Is one million a lot? Moral of the story: None of these statistics are interesting without some form of comparison. For instance, the Taj Mahal attracts 7-8 million tourists per year, Empire State Building 4 million, Tower of London 2 million.

11-13 These are all interesting and strange statistics that are likely to get the audience's attention. 11) Unless you are giving a medical presentation where statistics on deaths are common, giving information on suicide may attract audience attention, but in a rather morbid negative way. 12) This is a great statistic – it probably doesn't need a form of comparison as clearly the number of articles is huge. 13) Quirky (i.e. strange).

8.6 Statistics. What kind of statistics do audiences like? (cont.)

What is really needed in this case is a comparison with one other building, such as the Eiffel Tower in Paris. This will then put the statistics in a context and help the audience understand whether we are talking about relatively big numbers or small numbers.

When choosing your statistics, create a list of five or more statistics. Show them to colleagues, friends, and family, and get them to vote on the 2-3 that they find the most interesting. Choose the ones that were voted for by the most people. This should ensure that what you have chosen is interesting and relevant for your audience.

Choose one of the topics below and find three interesting statistics about them.

- Your country.
- Your hometown.
- Your hobby / personal interest.
- Your favorite movie / album.
- A member of your family.

Then create a short presentation on your topic + statistics. Decide whether you need slides to make your presentation more interesting and easier to follow.

8.7 Statistics. How should I present them on my slides?

Please look at the previous section (8.6), before doing this one.

More than 40,000 scientific papers have been written about the Leaning Tower of Pisa. Most of these are about the engineering problems involved in stopping the tower leaning so far that it will not fall down.

Imagine that you are a structural engineer and that you are going to present your work on the Leaning Tower. You have decided to begin your presentation with some statistics about the tower in comparison with the Eiffel Tower in Paris. Which of the following three slides do you think would be the most effective in getting the audience interested in your topic? Why?

SLIDE 1

True or False?

In relation to the Leaning Tower, the Eiffel Tower
1. is six times taller
2. weighs one third less
3. changes height by 15 cm in summer
4. attracts seven times as many tourists
5. costs less to climb

8.7 Statistics. How should I present them on my slides? (cont.)

SLIDE 2

1. Designed by Bonanno Pisano
2. Construction begins in 1173 (ends 1370)
3. 14,5000 tonnes
4. 55.86 m high
5. 294 steps
6. It leaned 5.5 degrees in 1990
7. One million tourists per year	1. Designed for Paris Expo
2. Intended to be demolished 1909
3. Weighs 10,000 tonnes. The paint weighs as much as 10 elephants
4. 320 m high (highest building for 41 years)
5. Lift cables cut when Hitler visited so he had to walk up the 1665 steps
6. Height varies by 15 cm due to temperature changes
7. 6.98 million (most visited paid monument in the world)

SLIDE 3

	Pisa	Paris
Designed	Bonanno Pisano	Designed for Paris Expo
Weight	14,5000	10,000
Height	55.86 m	320 m (highest building for 41 years)
Steps	294	1665
Changes	5.5 degrees in 1990	Height varies by 15 cm due to temperature changes
Tourists	1,000,000	6,980,000
Cost	€25	€15

8.7 Statistics. How should I present them on my slides? (cont.)

Always present statistics in a way that it is easy and quick for the audience to understand them (and possibly remember them). You don't want the audience to:

- spend too much time reading them (Slides 2 and 3)
- make too much mental effort absorbing them because the way they are presented is confusing (Slide 2 – the two sets of statistics are not aligned between points 2 and 5)
- get bored by your explanation of them (Slides 2 and 3 – what are you going to say about these two slides without just repeating the information?)

For me (and for nearly all my students who have seen these slides), Slide 1 is the best. Why?

- It contains much less info than the other two slides.
- It doesn't just give the audience info; it makes them think about the info before they are given the answers.
- It is more aesthetically pleasing than the other two. Slide 2 in particular looks very unprofessional.

The True or False approach is a great way to get audience attention. First you show the slide. Then you wait 4-5 seconds for the audience to think of the answers. Finally, you give them the answers. They will be much more motivated to listen to you if you have made them actively participate.

If you use this approach, make sure that the answers are not too difficult to guess. If they are too difficult, the audience may feel stupid and have a negative reaction towards you and your presentation.

8.8 Statistics. Can I put different sets of statistics on the same slide?

The slide below comes from a presentation on how obesity has a negative impact on the heart.

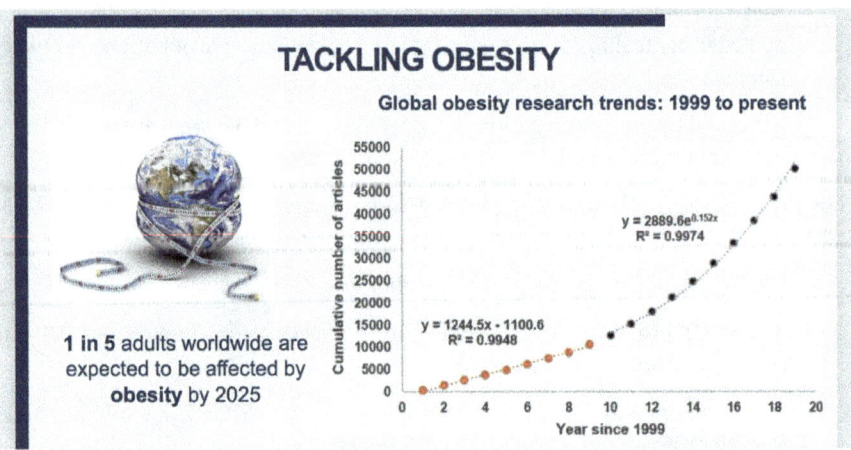

When we look at the slide, we see the number on the left (1 in 5 adults) and then we see a graph. Few people actually look at the legends on the x and y axis, and so the audience might presume that the graph shows the exponential rise of obesity cases. In fact, it refers to the numbers of research papers given on the topic.

Moral of the story: Each slide should have its own focus. If you put two pieces of info on the same slide, the audience might naturally assume that they are directly related.

8.8 Statistics. Can I put different sets of statistics on the same slide? (cont.)

Solution: Split the slide into two slides. Have a heading that clear reflects the topic of the slide. These two solutions are shown below (but read the following subsection regarding the misleading info shown in the first slide below).

OBESITY – AN INCREASING HEALTH COST

1 in 5 adults worldwide are expected to be affected by **obesity** by 2025

OBESITY: NUMBER OF RESEARCH ARTICLES SINCE 1999

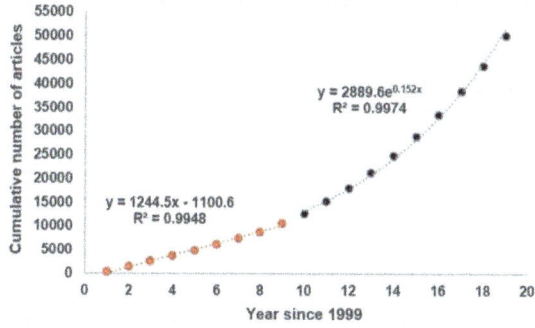

8.9 Misleading or unclear statistics. What do I need to be aware of?

The presenter of the obesity presentation (8.8) gives the following statistic:

1 in 5 adults worldwide are expected to be affected by obesity by 2025.

On the basis of the statistic, which of the following do you think are true?

- 1 in 5 adults **in my country** will be affected by obesity by 2025.
- 1 in 5 adults **in all countries** will be affected by obesity by 2025.
- 1 in 5 adults **in some countries** will be affected by obesity by 2025.

The term *worldwide* is very generic. It seems that all countries will have approximately 1 in 5 adults affected by obesity. But different countries have very different levels of obesity. For example, in the UK in 2020 67% of men and 60% of women were either overweight or obese. In 2017 the prevalence in obesity was 42.4%. One in five means 20%, so the US and UK levels are substantially higher than the world average. In China the obesity rates are between 5% and 6% in the country, and greater than 20% in towns (due to consumption of fast food). So *1 in 5* is totally misleading. A table of various countries might be more useful in this case. Such a table would also highlight that the urgency and risks associated with obesity vary considerably from country to country.

The presenter could also highlight the importance of her research by mentioning that 8% of global deaths are now caused by obesity.

Sources of the statistics given above:https://digital.nhs.uk; https://www.cdc.gov/obesity/data/adult.html#; en.wikipedia.org/wiki/Obesity_in_China; https://ourworldindata.org/obesity

I am English. I am often asked about my opinion of the Royal Family and how many British citizens would prefer to have a republic. Which ONE of the following would give you the clearest answer to the question?

1. A lot of people would like to replace the royal family with a republic.
2. 8.2 million people would rather have a republic.
3. 18% of the population would vote to abolish the Royal Family.

8.9 Misleading or unclear statistics. What do I need to be aware of? (cont.)

1) *a lot of* is a very vague term and will be interpreted very differently by different people. Always try to use a specific number.

2) *8.2 million* is a very specific number, but it is still unclear / misleading. If the total population is ten million then this is a huge number. If the population is 100 million, then it is only 8.2% of the population. When you give a number, you always need to put it in context. In this case the context is the total population.

3) 18% gives a precise indication. However, it could be made more interesting by telling the audience that the percentage was the same in 1969, in 1993, in 2002, in 2011 etc. ... basically, it doesn't seem to change. The statistic could be even more revealing if the audience were told how many citizens in other countries that have a monarchy would like to abolish it.

Chapters 8 (Methodology) and 9 (Results and Discussion), *English for Presentations at International Conferences*

Chapter 9
The visual aspect of slides

9.1 Slide sorter. How can I get an overall view of my presentation?

Look at the three presentations below. Based ONLY on their visual appearance, which presentation would you like to see the most? Why?

PRESENTATION 1

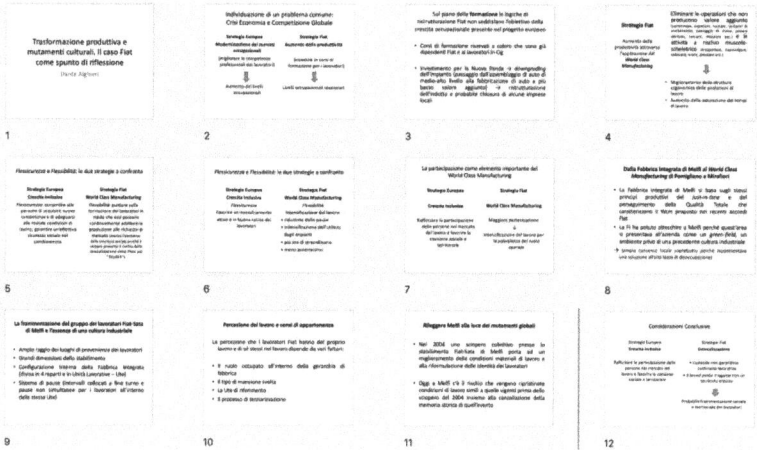

9.1 Slide sorter. How can I get an overall view of my presentation? (cont.)

PRESENTATION 2

PRESENTATION 3

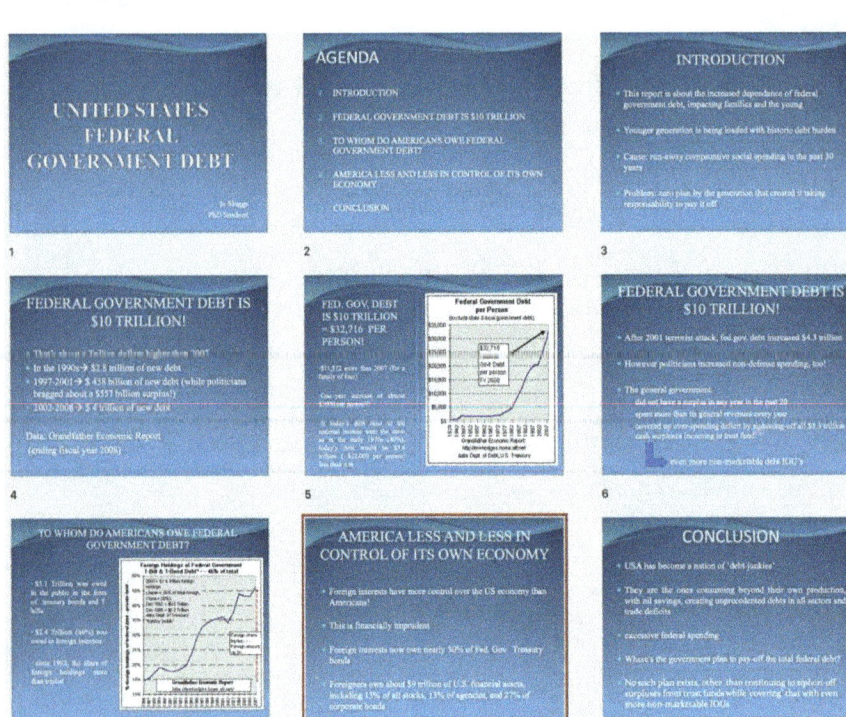

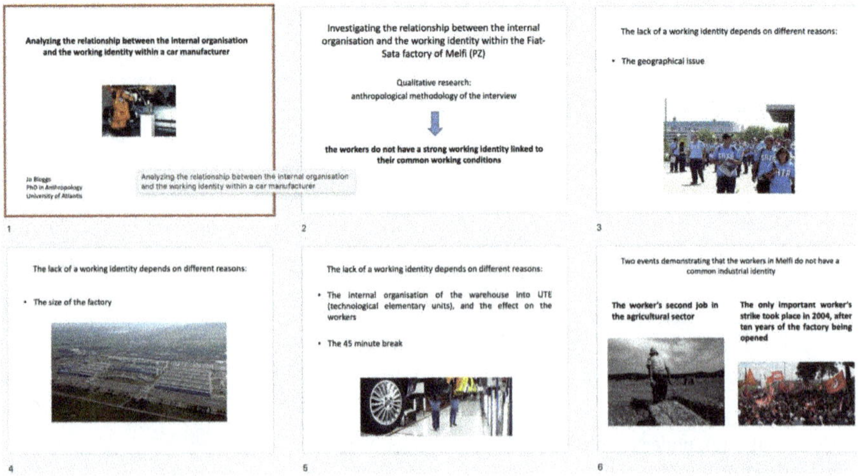

9.1 Slide sorter. How can I get an overall view of my presentation? (cont.)

If you use the 'slide sorter' option (under the menu 'view' in PowerPoint) you can see all your slides together, as illustrated on the previous pages.

Presentation 1: the slider sorter highlights that all your slides are text. This is unattractive for the audience. The slides also need something visual to provide variety and interest.

Presentation 2: the slider sorter highlights that the template is repeated throughout the entire presentation. Although to some people this may look professional, for some people in the audience it may be tedious. The slides all look the same and thus seem to all have the same importance.

Presentation 3 is a mix of text and images. It looks more visually appealing and is more likely to attract and maintain audience attention.

So use the slide sorter to get an overall view of our presentation. You will thus understand the overall visual impact that your presentation is likely to have.

9.2 Text. How can I limit the amount the number of words in a slide?

Look at the slide below. What is the problem with the text? How could it be improved?

Goals

- Development of a brand-new embedded magnets localizer that overcomes state-of-the-art ones limits
- Development of posture and activity recognition algorithms for myokinetic prosthetics control
- Investigation of external disturbance rejection strategies for a real-world scenario
- Investigation of power consumption optimization strategies

The phrases in the slide are incomplete from a grammatical point – there are no verbs. This is fine when you create bullet points. The problems are:

- because there is a lot of detail in the slide, there is little for the presenter to add. So he/she may be tempted just to read out the text, which for audiences is not very stimulating
- there are a lot of redundant words or words that give no information (*development, investigation*). And what is the difference between *new* and *brand-new*? and in any case if you are presenting new research, it should be obvious that something that overcomes current limitations must be new.

Your slides need to contain <u>just enough</u> text to enable:

- your audience to follow what you are saying
- you to remember what you have to say

9.2 Text. How can I limit the amount the number of words in a slide? (cont.)

The slide could thus be rewritten as follows:

- Embedded magnets localizer
- Posture + activity recognition algorithms
- External disturbance rejection strategies
- Optimized power consumption

Research has proved that most people's eyes focus on the first words and last words of a sentence / text. This means that you should put your key words as close as possible to the beginning of the sentence. Words such as *development* and *investigation* are very unspecific and thus not useful for the audience.

Your job is thus to explain how these key words relate to your research. You are not READING your slides. Instead, you are INTERPRETING them and ADDING information to them.

The slide below is from a presentation on the importance of making back up files.

Choosing the type of data to back up

- DOCUMENTS OF A PERSONAL NATURE
1. First, you need to prioritize documents that are not easy to replace. For example, you should make regular back up copies of wills, bank records, and any other financial data, private letters or personal files.

Redesign the slide above:

- reduce the amount text
- adjust the size of the headings
- think of ways to improve the bullets and to improve the overall visual impact

9.2 Text. How can I limit the amount the number of words in a slide? (cont.)

Look at the slide below. What improvements have been made?

Back Ups

Personal data: irreplaceable docs
- Wills
- Financial records
- Private letters
- Personal files

The text has been reduced considerably and the header is much shorter (*Back Ups* instead of *Choosing the type of data to back up*). Consequently, it is much quicker and easier for the audience to read. It also allows the presenter to say something (i.e. to comment on the bullet points), whereas in the original slide which used a complete sentence, the only option for the presenter would be to read the sentence aloud.

9.3 Headers/Slide titles. How big should they be?

The four slides below all contain the same information.

Which of the four slides do you like the best? Why? What are the problems with the other three?

SLIDE 1

> **Back Ups**
>
> **Personal data: irreplaceable docs**
> • Wills
> • Financial records
> • Private letters
> • Personal files

SLIDE 2

> **Back Ups**
>
> **Personal data: irreplaceable docs**
> • Wills
> • Financial records
> • Private letters
> • Personal files

SLIDE 3

> **Back Ups**
>
> **Personal data: irreplaceable docs**
> • Wills
> • Financial records
> • Private letters
> • Personal files

9.3 Headers/Slide titles. How big should they be? (cont.)

SLIDE 4

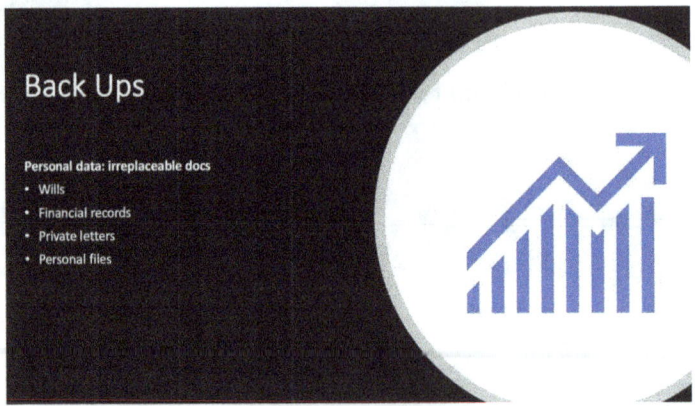

Slide 1 is very clear but looks a little like a cut&paste from a Word document. It also gives the impression that the presenter did not try very hard to make his / her slides attractive for the audience. The presenter may thus lose a little credibility.

Slide 2 highlights the problem with most presentation software: it encourages you to have very big titles for each slide. To me, it makes much more sense to have the important information, rather than the title/heading, in a bigger font. In some cases, the title may be the most important element in a slide, but often it is not.

Slide 3 is the best. The title is smaller, but the key information is bigger and clearer for the audience.

Slide 4 highlights another issue with presentation software. If you use the 'Design Ideas' feature (which is often really great) it often proposes a massive symbol that may occupy more than 50% of the slide. It also reduces the font size of your text. If you like the symbol, then at least increase the size of the text. Also, note that having a dark background doesn't look good when printed.

9.4 Design Ideas: Are they useful?

PowerPoint and other presentation software have a function called 'Design Ideas'. You create your slide, then press the button (circled in the screenshot below).

Look at the nine Design Ideas suggestions below.

a) Which two are the most effective? And the two least effective?

b) Is it possible to state objectively which one is the best?

c) Generally speaking, which colors do you think work best in combination?

d) Generally speaking, which do you think are the best and worst fonts to use in a presentation?

There is no key to this exercise.

1

9.4 Design Ideas: Are they useful? (cont.)

2

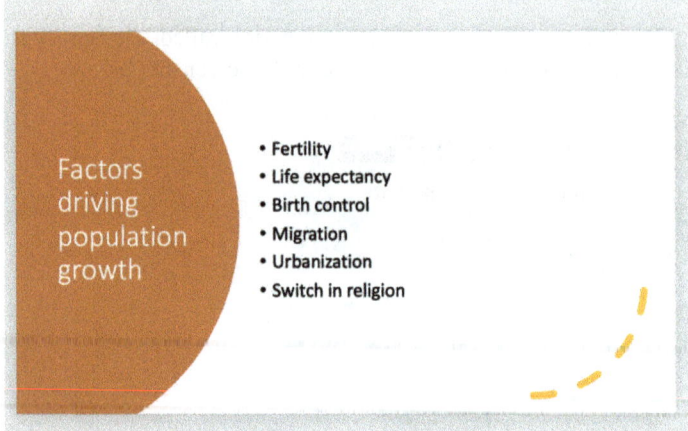

3

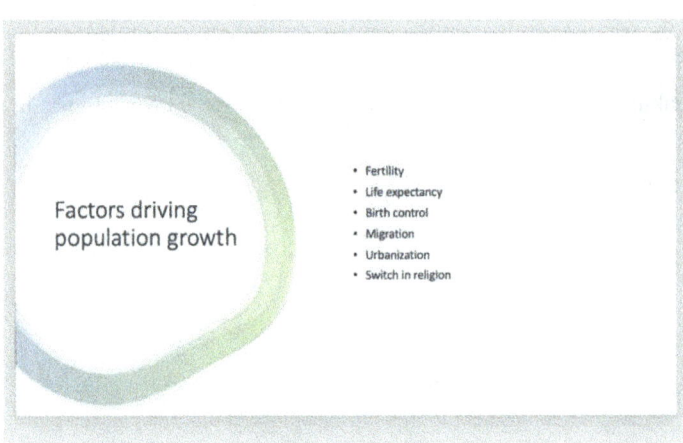

9.4 Design Ideas: Are they useful? (cont.)

4

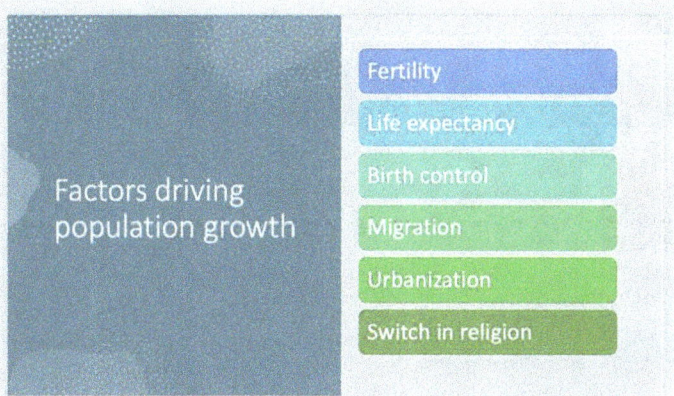

5

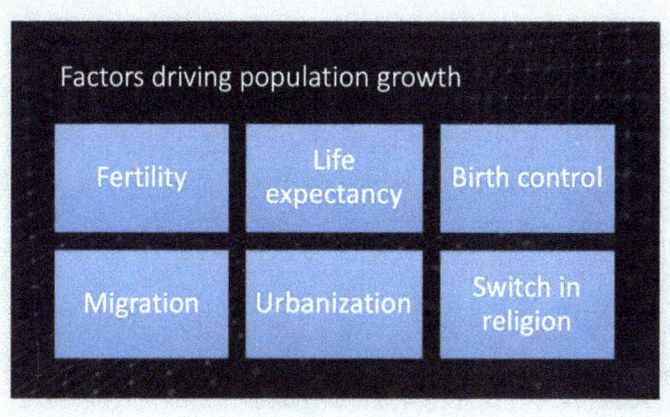

9.4 Design Ideas: Are they useful? (cont.)

6

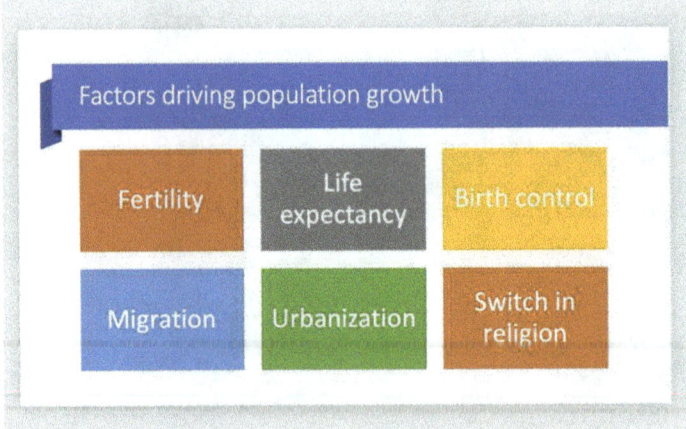

7

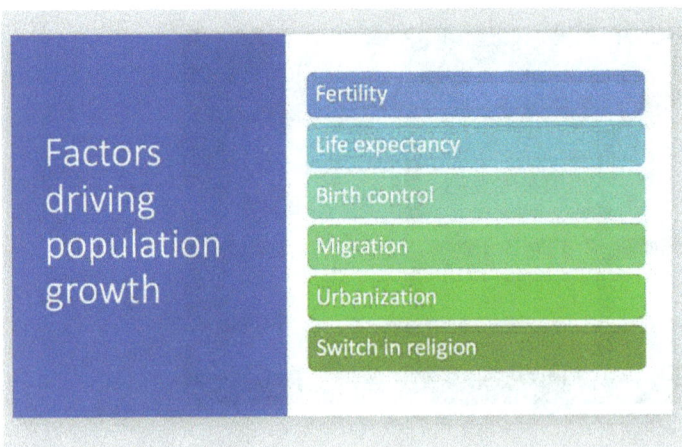

9.4 Design Ideas: Are they useful? (cont.)

8

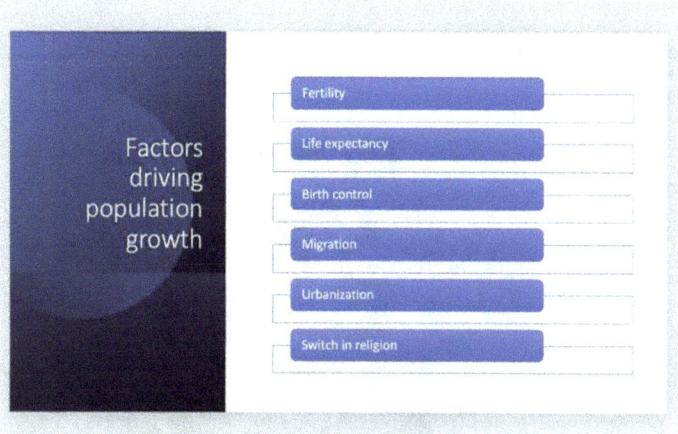

9

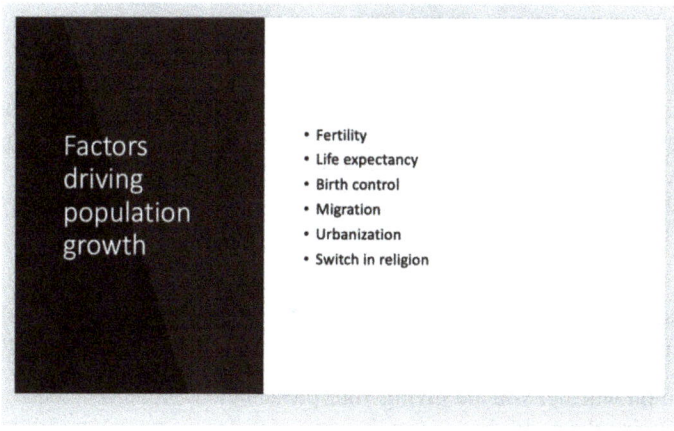

9.4 Design Ideas: Are they useful? (cont.)

'Design Ideas' tends to give a lot of emphasis to titles and images, as in the example below.

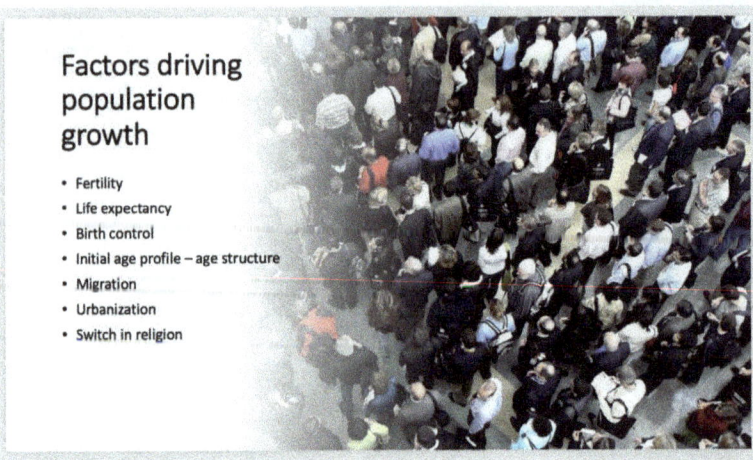

This means that your bullet points may be very small. This is not helpful because the bullet points are precisely what you want your audience to focus on: not the heading or image. Consequently, 1 and 5 are not audience friendly.

'Design Ideas' is a fantastic tool for making your presentation look professional. However, your priority is clarity for the audience, rather than simply 'looking good'.

Much will depend on whether you are giving your presentation online or in person at a conference. Online the slide above may be very small for the person watching on a laptop, so the bullet points may be hard to read. However, on a big screen at a live conference, the fact that the photograph dominates the slide would not be a problem.

9.5 Building a sequence of slides. I want to repeat an element from one slide in the next slide. How should I do this?

In the three slides below, the presenter is talking about the growth of population in a town, starting from its origins to today. He has used a typical way of building up information. The presenter has 'duplicated' his first slide in his second and third slides. But in the third slide he has added a graph showing the population levels in this town of the years. The result is that the graph is very difficult to read for the audience.

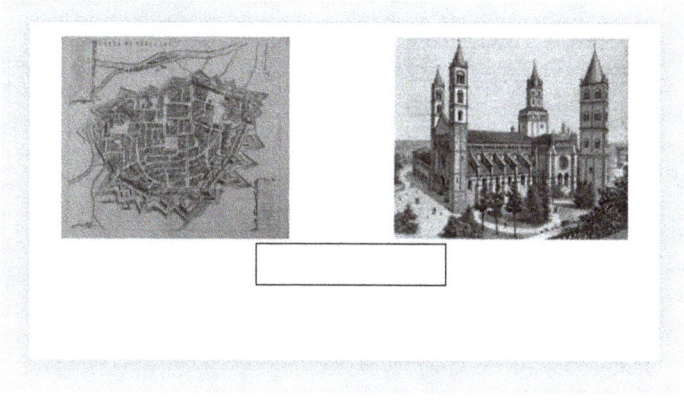

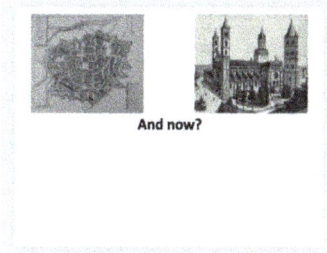

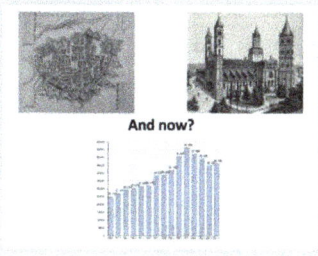

9.5 Building a sequence of slides. I want to repeat an element from one slide in the next slide. How should I do this? (cont.)

A better solution for the third slide is:

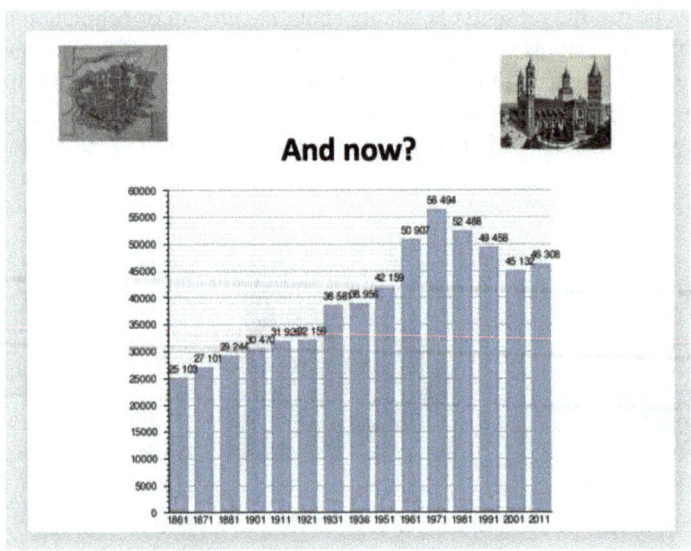

In this new version of slide 3, the two images, which the audience have seen in the previous two slides and are consequently now of less importance as they give OLD information, have been reduced in size. This means that the graph can be made much more readable.

Note: In the slide above, the last year mentioned is 2011, which is many years ago. This gives the impression of incomplete information and that the presenter could not be bothered to find the most recent data. This could frustrate the audience and undermine the presenter's credibility.

If you can't an up-to-date graph then you can simply say: *The population in 2011 was just over 46,000, since then the population has dropped again, and is now approximately 40,000.*

9.6 What kind of slides are overused and thus have little effect? Cartoons?

Look at the three slides below.

1. Have you ever seen them before or something similar?
2. Do you like them? Why (not)?
3. How do you think someone 10, 20, 30 years older than you might answer the previous two questions?

Presentations frequently contain slides similar to the ones above. The effect they will have will often depend on not just on the taste / opinion of the audience, but also how old they are. The older they are, the more likely they have seen slides like the ones above. Such slides are not original and are thus not likely to draw much attention from the audience.

Don't use assume that the audience will automatically appreciate them.

For a good analysis on the use of cartoons (such as in the third slide above), see:

https://graphicmama.com/blog/using-cartoons-in-presentations/

9.6 What kind of slides are overused and thus have little effect? Cartoons? (cont.)

The cartoon below was created for a textbook on how to teach English to non-native speakers of English. The first character is the teacher, the others are students. Don't worry if you can't read the text very well, I just want you to focus on the pictures.

Note: there are some non-deliberate mistakes in the English – *isa, choses*.

1. Do you like the cartoon in terms of how the people are drawn, i.e. the style?

2. Do you think everyone in your class / family / institute would share your opinion?

3. Do you think Chinese woman and Japanese man (in the fourth image) would be able to associate with how they are visually depicted in the cartoon?

4. In general, how risky is it to use cartoons (funny ones, and non-humorous ones like the one above)?

5. Is humor international?

9.6 What kind of slides are overused and thus have little effect? Cartoons? (cont.)

The problem with all kinds of cartoons is that some people will love them, some will be indifferent, and some will actively not look them. It is difficult to predict how your audience will react.

Humor is a great part of presentations. But be very careful not to offend anyone. A safe kind of humor, which most audiences will appreciate, is when you make fun of yourself or of problems you may have had during your research.

9.7 Should I use fun images?

The three slides below are the first three slides of a presentation on how plants can sense sounds. The structure of the slides is very clear: Slide 1 Title, Slide 2 Introduction, Slide 3 goal. The audience will certainly be able to follow this presentation without difficulty.

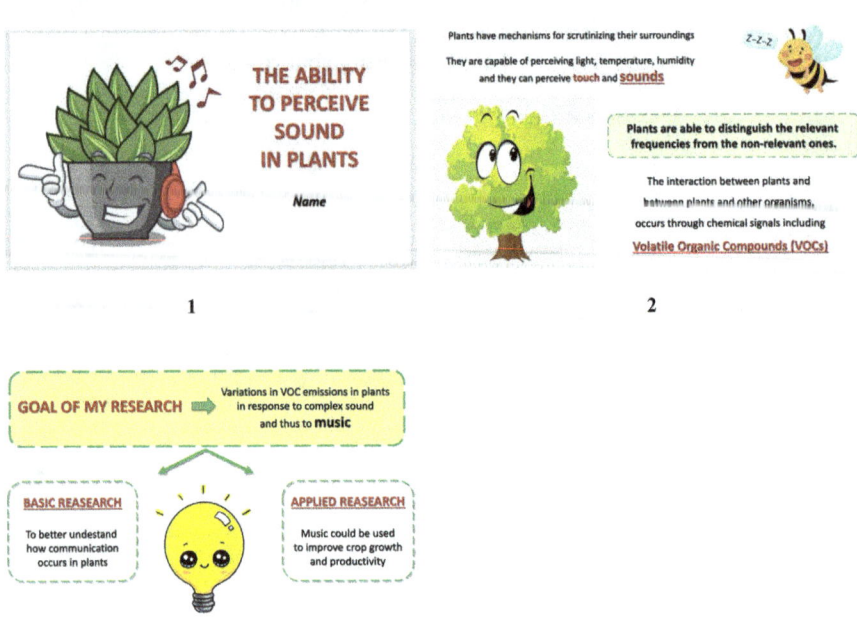

1. The images are fun, but are they appropriate for an academic presentation?

2. What kind of audience would appreciate such fun images?

3. For an academic audience, what images might be more suitable?

4. Generally speaking, are fun images a good idea? How might a presentation benefit from having one or two light / humorous images?

9.7 Should I use fun images? (cont.)

1. An entire presentation made up of images of this type is unlikely to impress many members of an academic audience. One such image is probably enough.
2. Children at school.
3. More serious images would be appropriate. The problem is that these kinds of images are so frequent on the internet that they lose impact and possibly undermine the credibility of the presenter. I think Slide 1 is fine as it is – it's fun and will make the audience feel relaxed. However, in Slide 2 the bee could be removed, and the tree replaced with a real tree or a scientific diagram of a tree. The lightbulb in Slide 3 has been overused in presentations – audiences have seen it so many times. This slide could just have a few musical notes.
4. See below.

Humor is cultural. What is fun / funny in your culture, may not be universally funny. When you use what you consider to be a humorous slide, think about the following:

- Could this image possibly offend someone of another i) nationality; ii) gender; iii) race / ethnicity / religion?
- Is this image in fact just funny for me? In reality, am I just pleased with myself for having found this image and having found a way to use it in my presentation?

When you have decided what YOU think it is suitable, show it to as many colleagues as possible to check their opinion. Ensure you also show it to colleagues who are not your nationality in case it might be offensive for reasons that you could not have possibly known.

9.8 Restrictions on the number of slides that can be used. What to do?

Sometimes you are given a restriction on the number of slides you can use. The result is that you may be tempted to produce crowded slides like the following:

SLIDE 1

Topic:
Build models quantitative structure-activity relationship (QSAR) of deep learning utilizing DeepChem project software understand the functionality and matching the deep learning models with the QSAR standard models.
Overview of the project:
The objective of the project was to use the python based module 'DeepChem' to build and validate models of QSAR for small molecules. The results of these models will be eventually compared with other standard QSAR models.
Skills acquired:

- Understanding Deep Learning
- Usage of DeepChem module
- Understanding of Neural Network models
- Develop a functional python code
- Test code on publicly available data on small molecules
- Implement hyper-parameter optimization

SLIDE 2

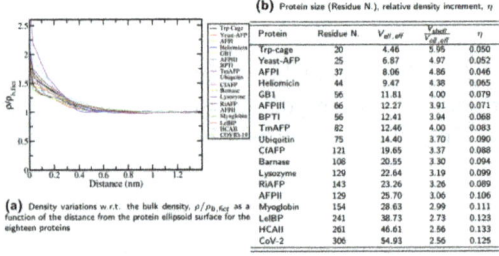

9.8 Restrictions on the number of slides that can be used. What to do? (cont.)

SLIDE 3

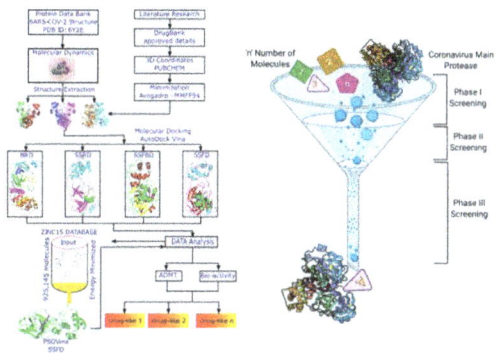

Drug Screening for CoV-2 Main Protease

The first slide has three separate subjects – topic, overview, and skills acquired. These would be much better presented in three separate slides.

The second and third slides each have two separate subjects. So, in this case, two slides would be clearer.

The problem with all three slides is that the audience has too much to look at, and in any case they will not all be looking at the same parts at the same time. You will thus divide the audience's attention.

For example, in the first slide, the audience will be reading much faster than you are speaking. So maybe you are still speaking about the 'Topic', but the audience are reading about 'Skills acquired'. Consequently, they may not hear what you say about 'Topic', and may simply stop listening because they have read as much as they want.

In the second and third slides you cannot guarantee where the audience will focus their eyes: on the left? on the right? at the top? at the bottom?

A good presenter is totally in synchronism with the audience. This means that all the audience is focusing on the same thing at the same time, i.e. they are all looking at the same part of the same diagram, or they are all listening to what you are saying (rather than some listening and some reading).

If you can only use a very limited number of your slides, you will inevitably lose this synchronism.

9.8 Restrictions on the number of slides that can be used. What to do? (cont.)

If you have a restricted number of slides, do NOT simply compact your normal 10-slide presentation into three slides. Accept that you CANNOT and SHOULD NOT try to present the same amount of information.

Imagine you can only have three slides. Follow this procedure:

1. Remove everything that you can from your original 10 slides – this will probably be easier than you imagine.
2. Decide on three points that the audience absolutely MUST hear /see.
3. Put these three points on three separate slides.
4. Ensure that these three slides are easy for the audience to understand and easy for you to explain.
5. Tell the audience that if they need more information, your full presentation (see the second half of 8.2) is available for download (so you need to upload your full presentation on your home page, on your institute's website, on LinkedIn etc.).

With this procedure you have resolved the problem!

In reality, having more slides does NOT mean a longer presentation. You can have five slides and spend two minutes on each, ten slides and one minute, or twenty slides and thirty seconds – in total the time you spend will be 10 minutes in each case. The more slides you have, generally the easier it is for the audience to absorb the information. This is because each slide can contain one key idea. Having more slides also makes a presentation more dynamic and helps maintain audience attention.

Rather than putting a limit on the number of slides, it thus makes much more sense to put a limit on the time. Unfortunately, some organizers don't seem to understand this. The result is a limited number of slides packed with information that is difficult for the presenter to explain and for the audience to absorb.

Chapter 5 (Visual Elements and Fonts), *English for Presentations at International Conferences*

Chapter 10
The conclusions and final slide

10.1 How should I present my conclusions?

The last two slides of a presentation are typically:

- a Conclusions slide, where the presenter summarizes the key points of his/her presentation
- a Final slide, which signals that the presentation has nearly ended, and where the presenter leaves his/her contact details, asks if anyone has any questions (though the conference chair may ask this), and thanks the audience

Sometimes these two slides are combined into one slide as in the example below:

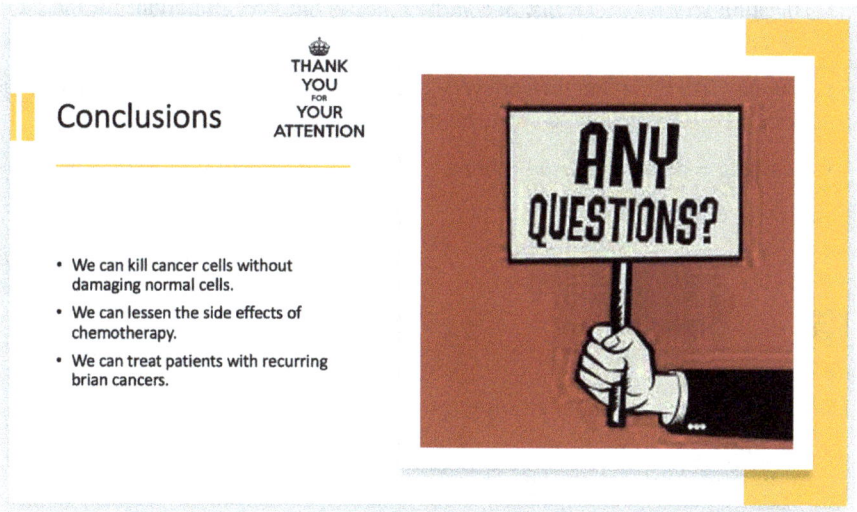

10.1 How should I present my conclusions? (cont.)

Look at the slide on the previous page and the script below. The presenter is presenting her conclusions and ending her presentation.

There are three main benefits of our method. Firstly, we can kill cancer cells without damaging normal cells. Secondly, the side effects of chemotherapy can be lessened. Finally, our treatment can be useful in treating patients who have had recurrent brain cancers. Thank you for attention. If you have any questions, I will happy be happy to answer them.

1. Which parts of the script are effective and useful for the audience?
2. Do you like the two images (*Thank you ... Any Questions?*)?
3. Can you spot two spelling mistakes in the slide?

1) The summary parts (*Firstly, Secondly, Finally*) are very important for the audience to hear. They are reminders of the three key points that the presenter has made.

2) You may like them, but they are very over-used and will have little impact on the audience (see 10.3 on how to create an impact).

3) *recurring* = recurrent; *brian* = brain.

*****

Look back at the slide and the script.

1. Does the script add anything that the audience couldn't understand by simply reading the slide in silence?
2. Instead, what could the presenter say about each of the three bullet points?

10.1 How should I present my conclusions? (cont.)

1) No. 2) See below.

When you are presenting bullet points (8.4., 8.5, 9.2), don't simply read or paraphrase the text in the bullets. Do not repeat the text on your slide. Instead, expand on it or explain it further. First let the audience read the text, then select one or more bullet points to talk about in more detail.

Below is a more effective script for describing the three points on the slide.

So there are three main benefits of our method. *Pauses to let audience read the text*. Firstly, by not damaging the normal cells they remain healthy, which is crucial because ... Secondly, we can reduce side effects such as hair loss, nausea, and infection. Finally, between 24% and 32% of patients have recurrent brain cancers. So our treatment stops a new meningioma from growing in the same spot.

10.2 How can I connect my Conclusions slide with my Final slide?

Below are two sets of slides (set 1 and set 2).

In each case the slide on the left is the Conclusions, i.e. the penultimate slide of the presentation, where the presenter summarizes his / her work. The slide on the right is the last slide that the audience will see.

Both sets of slides are skeleton slides, i.e. they are not complete and the headings are designed to show you the function of each slide – they would not be used in the real presentation. The slides could also contain some images.

The letters (P, Q, R and X, Y, Z) refer to some research issue.

In terms of structure, how effective do you think this sequence of two slides is?

SET 1

Conclusion slide

What we've done so far:
- P
- Q
- R

What we still need to do:
- X
- Y
- Z

Final slide

Do you have X?
What is your experience with Y?
Can you help us with Z?

jo.bloggs@institute.com

10.2 How can I connect my Conclusions slide with my Final slide? (cont.)

SET 2

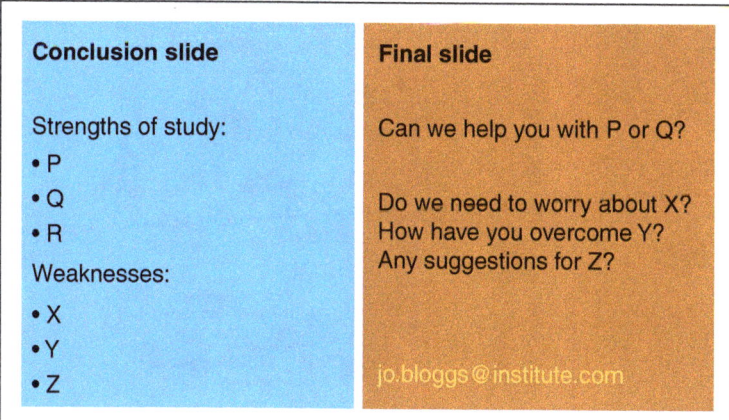

✎

The slides above need to be amplified with details. But they are a concise and effective way to use your conclusions as a way to ask your audience questions.

On the next page is an example of the Conclusions and Final slide of a very technical presentation entitled *Integrity control of blockchain based documents*. Don't worry about the topic or the actual content of the slide, but simply note how the presenter uses his SWOT analysis (Strengths, Weaknesses, Opportunities, Threats) to try to elicit help from the audience. Specifically, he repeats the last sentence from the Threats (bottom right) in his final slide.

10.2 How can I connect my Conclusions slide with my Final slide? (cont.)

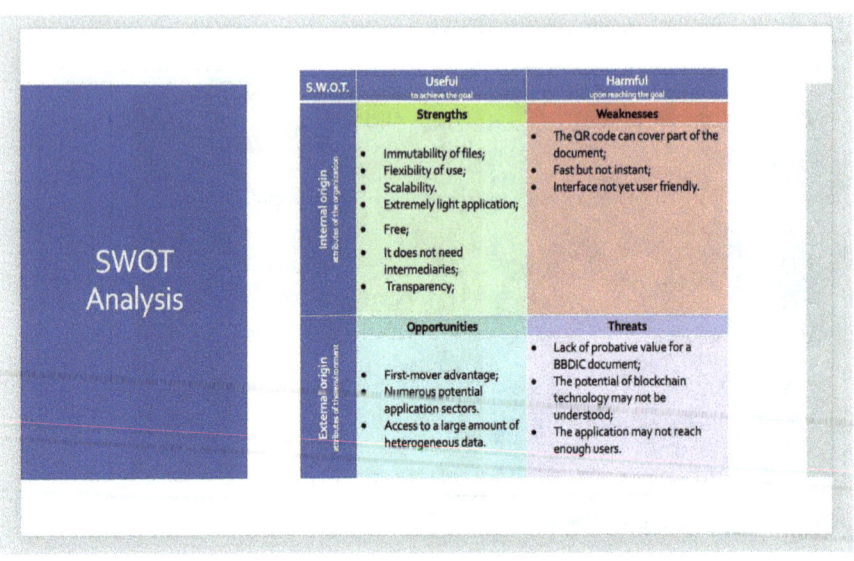

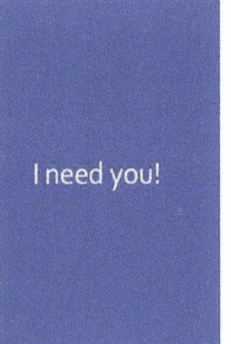

10.3 What is the real purpose of the final/last slide of my presentation?

1. How often have you seen slides like the ones above, i.e. which simply say *Thank you for your attention*? How memorable for the audience is such a slide? What purpose does it serve? Do the images (dominoes, smiley) serve any purpose?
2. What do YOU typically write on YOUR final slide?
3. What images, if any, do you put?
4. What logos and acknowledgements do you put? What is their purpose?
5. What information do you think the audience might want to see?
6. Can you spot the mistakes in the two slides?

1) Slides like these are used to end many presentations. But because they are so common, they have no positive impact on the audience and will not help the audience to remember the presentation. The images, too, are very common and instantly forgettable.

2) Write your email address in big letters, along with reasons why the audience should contact you (10.4).

3) If you use an image, make sure it relates to your presentation or to you or to your research team (10.4). It should not just be a random image.

4) If your research is being sponsored, you may be legally obliged to put the sponsor's logo. Your university / institute may also require you to put their logo. In both cases, you don't want the logos to be too prominent as they are not of great interest to your audience. The same applies to the people that you acknowledge. Of course if your sponsors and the people you wish to acknowledge are important or known to the audience or wish to see their names in big print, then you should do what you can to please them.

10.3 What is the real purpose of the final/last slide of my presentation? (cont.)

5) See 2 above. Plus they might want to know how to download your presentation, where to find your publications, where you are located, what you plan to do next in your research.

6) Slide 1: *Thank you for your attention.* Slide 2: *tanks; your your*

The aim of your last slide is to:

- Help the audience **remember** you (1.7)
- Initiate **collaborations** (1.1)
- Encourage them to **contact** you (10.4)

10.4 Why should I want the audience to contact me? How do I do so?

Below is the final slide of a presentation by a medical doctor, Luigi Pallino, who is based in Pisa, which is in the region of Tuscany, Italy.

Top left: research team in the lab. Top right: a typical panorama in Tuscany – Italy's most famous region. Bottom left: the Leaning of Tower of Pisa (Tuscany) where the research lab is based. Bottom right: x, y and z refer to research problems.

1. In what ways (text and photos) do you think the above slide is designed to get people to contact Luigi?

2. How effective do you think it is?

3. Would / Could you try to do something similar? How? (If not, why not?)

10.4 Why should I want the audience to contact me? How do I do so? (cont.)

Your presentation has no value if the audience simply get up when you have finished, leave the room (or turn off their computer), and forget everything they have heard. It might help you if you see your presentation as a product that you are trying to 'sell' to your audience (1.1). You thus need your audience to contact you to:

- find out more about your 'product' – maybe simply by asking for the relevant paper if you have published one
- offer to help you solve any difficulties you are having – by providing their experience and expertise
- help you improve your 'product' – by offering to collaborate with you, or let you use their facilities (equipment, data, library)

There are several ways to encourage the audience to contact you:

- Putting your email address in a prominent position in the slide
- A photo of your group (this gives the idea that you are supported by a friendly group of experienced researchers)
- A photo of the region / town where your lab is located (particularly if you live in a place that might be attractive for other researchers to visit)
- Provide reasons to contact you: you need their help (i.e. limitations to your research, equipment lacking in your lab etc. – see 10.5) or you think there may be ways that you can help them

10.5 How can I use the limitations of my research to possibly set up a collaboration?

1. Who is more credible and approachable: Someone with apparently no limitations, or someone who admits their limitations?
2. Do you think that admitting that your research has limitations is a weakness?
3. Which of the following are true for you?
   a) You don't have sufficient time to carry out all the tests you need to do.
   b) Old data – you need more recent data.
   c) You don't have access to particular libraries.
   d) Your sample size is too small or too restricted.
   e) You don't have sufficient funds.
   f) You don't have the right tools, substances, equipment.
   g) Bad weather prevents you from carrying out your research.
   h) You can't get authorization to do the tests that you want to do.
   i) You keep repeating your tests, but you get different results each time.
   j) So far you've only done *in vitro* tests, you need to do *in vivo* tests.
   k) You have texts that you need to read that are in a foreign language that you don't have knowledge of.

Below are some possible ways to use the limitations listed above (a-k) to enlist help from the audience. I have given you the exact words you could use. The phrase *it would be great if you could contact us* can be used to end all examples.

a) Our research is urgent but is taking too long. We simply don't have enough human resources. If you are working in the field of xyz *it would be great if you could contact us*.

b) Currently we only have data for up to three years ago. If you have any more recent data ...

c) Given where we are located / given the small size of our institute, we don't have access to xyz libraries. If on the other hand you do have access to these libraries ...

10.5 How can I use the limitations of my research to possibly set up a collaboration? (cont.)

d) Our research was confined to pqr, we really need to extend our sample to include xyz. If you have done any work on xyz …

e) As you know, this kind of research is expensive. We are looking for collaborators to see if we can share the costs …

f) Unfortunately we don't have xyz, if you do …

g) Our lab is located in an area that, due to climate change, is getting much less rain than before. If your lab is an area with at least 000 centimeters of rain per year …

h) If by any chance you have authorization for xyz …

i) It is a little frustrating as we seem to get different results every time. If you have any suggestions regarding why this happens …

j) Unfortunately we have been unable to do any in vivo tests yet because … if you could help us with this …

k) I am looking for a potential collaborator who speaks Wolof to help me do xyz. If you speak this language and are interested in collaborating with me …

Think about any limitations to your research. Then think about how other researchers might be able to overcome these limitations. Could a collaboration possibly result from your discussions with these researchers?

Studies have proved that unfortunately some researchers hide their limitations or are not transparent about what their data means (see, for instance, *Bad Science* by Dr Ben Goldacre). This can lead to misleading results.

Audiences like presenters who are honest about the difficulties they are encountering. This is something that all researchers can associate with and sympathize with. The fact that most presenters do not admit to such difficulties is not a reason for you not to do so. You can simply just ask for suggestions or, on the other hand, offer to help others.

By talking about your difficulties, you will also encourage people at the conference to talk to you about these difficulties during the social dinners or at the bar. They might say "So, you said that you are having problems with xyz. Have you thought about doing abc?" This is the perfect opportunity for a dialog to begin that might end up being a collaboration!

10.6 How can I improve my final slide?

1. Below are four final slides from four different presentations. In each case try to understand what the presenter is trying to do.
2. They are good slides. But they could be improved. How?

SLIDE 1

10.6 How can I improve my final slide? (cont.)

SLIDE 2

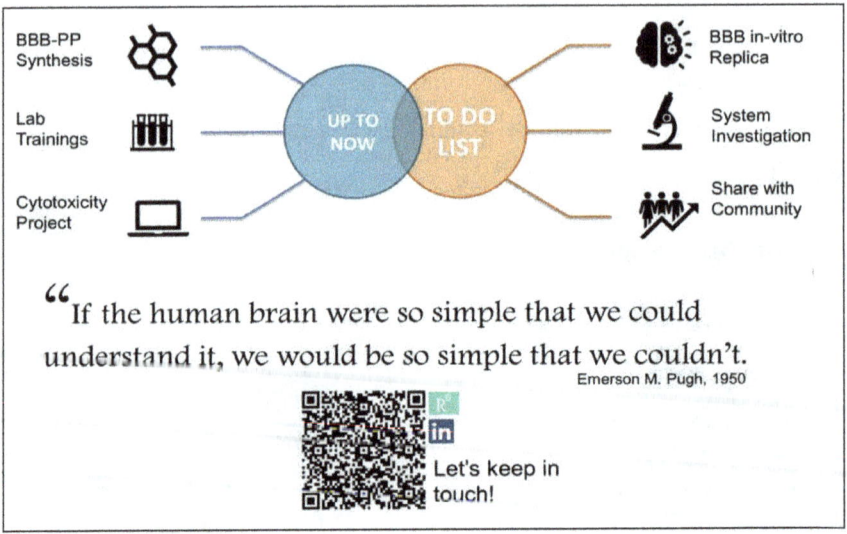

SLIDE 3

10.6 How can I improve my final slide? (cont.)

SLIDE 4

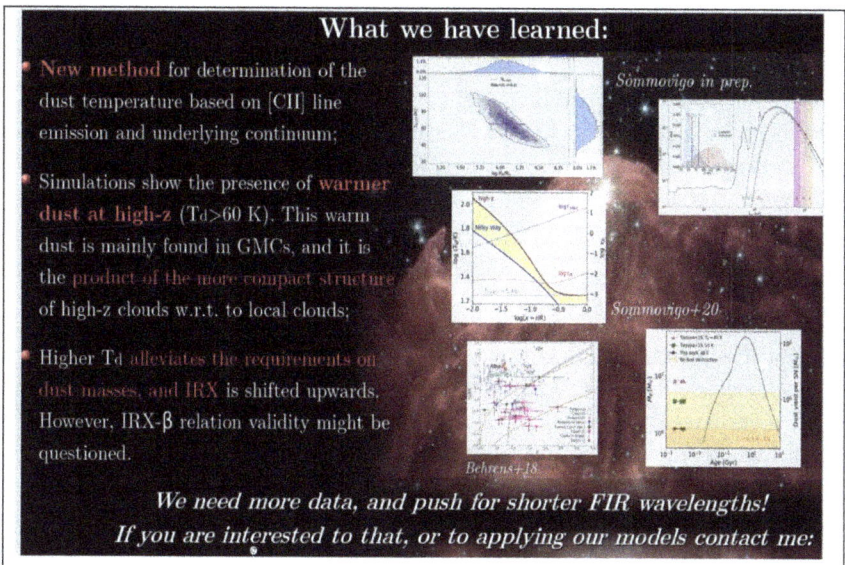

SLIDE 1 The slide works very well in terms of encouraging the audience to contact her through a series of question and by telling them about the website. The photo of the researcher's team gives the idea of the teamwork behind the research. The presenter's email is very prominent, which is good. Having the email means you can say: *if you would like to know more about my research please contact me at this email address.*

Drawbacks. The slide is very crowded. The Facebook and Instagram logos and details seem unnecessary. There are also a three logos. If the logos are of your sponsors, you may be obliged to put them. But if they are logos of your institute, they are unnecessary for the audience to see.

SLIDE 2 The *up to now* and *to do* list are a clever way of summarizing your presentation and at the same time telling the audience what you need to do next. The presenter can then use the *to do* list to elicit help from the audience. The QR code is a great way to enable your audience to get further information – provided of course that they can scan it with their phone. Scanning is certainly possible if you are doing the presentation online. If you are doing it face to face with your audience, you could tell them where they could download your presentation so that they could scan the QR code directly from the presentation file.

10.6 How can I improve my final slide? (cont.)

Drawbacks. There is no email contact address. The quotation from Pugh takes up a lot of space and is not instantly understandable. If the audience read it but don't understand it, then they will be left with a negative rather than positive impression. Quotations look good, but ensure that can be understood very easily.

SLIDE 3 She can use her two limitations to elicit help from the audience. It is OK to put a photo so that anyone who saw your presentation at a conference and has downloaded the online version will be reminded of you. In any case, make sure the photo is as professional as possible and does not distract or detract from the message of your presentation. Your content is obviously more important than your appearance.

Drawbacks. What is the point of the image on the left? Don't put images simply to fill a white space. Consider just making the other elements in the slide bigger.

SLIDE 4 If you work in a field where this kind of slide is a commonly used (online the audience can take a screenshot to remember the entire content of the presentation), then maybe you could use it too. But it might be best as your penultimate slide. Then in your final slide you can use some of the techniques used in Slides 1-3.

10.7 How important is the final/last slide of a presentation?

a) How many movies have you watched when the first 20 minutes were excellent, but the rest was mediocre and the ending very poor?

b) How many times have you watched a disappointing final episode of a great TV series?

c) What do you think is the connection between questions 1 and 2, and the feelings that an audience have when a presentation ends?

d) How important do you think your final slides are compared to i) the introductory slides, and ii) the technical slides?

Audiences don't usually have great expectations for the last slide of a presentation. Often such slides look very similar and the speaker simply says 'thank you'. This leaves the audience feeling indifferent and uninspired.

You will have spent a lot of preparing your presentation and possibly money on flying to a conference. So if the second you stop presenting, the audience forgets most of what you have said, you will have wasted an opportunity to get other researchers interested / involved in your research.

When you have finished your presentation, including the question-and-answer session (Chapter 11), it is customary to thank the audience. However there is no need to have a final slide that simply says 'Thank you for your attention'.

Chapter 10 (Conclusions), *English for Presentations at International Conferences*

Chapter 11
Q&A Session

11.1 I am nervous about the Q&A session. How can I prepare for it?

1. How worried are you about the Q&A session? a) not much b) normal c) very.
2. Are the questions that you might be asked out of your control (i.e. totally random)?
3. How can you predict the questions that the audience might ask you?

It is totally normal to be worried about the Q&A. It may seem that you have no control over the questions the audience might ask you. In reality you do have some control, as long as you give yourself time to prepare before the presentation. Practice your presentation in front of colleagues, friends, and relatives, and get them to write down three questions that they would like you to answer. Choose the ones that you think are the most relevant, then prepare answers to them.

If you have thought of all the questions your audience are likely to ask, it will enable you to

- seem professional in your immediate ability to answer a question
- stand a better chance of understanding (in terms of the words the questioner uses) such questions when they are asked
- prepare in advance extra slides to answer such questions
- prepare yourself mentally so that during the Q&A session you can remain calm

11.1 I am nervous about the Q&A session. How can I prepare for it? (cont.)

If you are very nervous about the Q&A session, a good solution is the following. If you are at a conference with a colleague, arrange with this colleague to ask you a question. If there are no colleagues with, choose someone that you have met at the conference who you like and who seems friendly. Ask him/her to ask you the first question.

In both cases you should tell them what question you want them to ask you. You could even have an extra slide that answers the question. This will make you look very professional and will give the audience a positive final impression.

Chapter 13 *Handling Your Nerves* in *English for Presentations at International Conferences*

11.2 How should I answer questions at an online conference?

If you understand the question or understand it partially, answer it following the suggestions given in 11.3.

If you don't understand the question because you did not / cannot hear it well, then say: *Sorry, my English is not great. Could you message me the question / post it on the chat.* If the questioner messages the question just to you, then read the question aloud so that the other participants can hear it. Then answer it.

If still you don't understand because you don't understand what they are asking or because you don't know the answer, then say: *That's a great question. Would you mind if I emailed you the answer as I need to check with a colleague first?* or something similar.

11.3 How should I answer questions at traditional offline conferences?

1. Is it a good idea to repeat the question before you answer it? Why (not)?
2. Do you tend to give short or long answers to questions? What are pros and cons of each approach?
3. If the question simply requires a 'yes' or 'no' answer, do you feel it is acceptable to simply answer 'yes' or 'no'?
4. If the question has two or more parts (i.e. multiple questions in the same question), what do you do?
5. What should you do if the questioner is taking a very long time to ask his/her question?
6. What can you do if the questioner seems to be trying to provoke you by being controversial?

1) If your audience is quite big, repeat the question so that the rest of the audience can hear it clearly. This is crucial if the question comes from someone in the front row, as the back rows will not be able to hear it. Repeating the question will also enable

- you to have time to think about an answer
- you to reformulate any contorted questions
- the questioner to check that you have understood their question

In any case, give yourself two to three seconds to formulate your answer before responding.

2, 3) Be concise, otherwise you might forget what the question was. If the question only requires the answer *yes* or *no*, be brief and move on to the next question. If you are tempted to begin a long conversation with someone in the audience, offer to meet up later.

4) Choose the part of the question that is simplest to answer. If you forget the other part of the question, you can ask them again, or move on to another question, and then go up to the person after the presentation and talk to them directly.

11.3 How should I answer questions at traditional offline conferences? (cont.)

5 Most people don't appreciate being interrupted when they are asking a question. However, if they are having difficulty in expressing themselves and you feel it would be right to help them, you could say, "So you are asking me if ..." or you could say: "This sounds like a really interesting question. But I think it might be best if you asked me it at the bar".

6) Don't be defensive; try to stay calm. Simply say: *I think you have raised an interesting point and it would be great if we could discuss it in the bar*. Or: *I was not aware of those findings. Perhaps you could tell me about them at the social dinner*. Some people just ask questions to demonstrate their own knowledge. In this case, you can say: *You are absolutely right. I didn't mention that point because it is quite technical/because there was no time. But it is covered in my paper*.

Give yourself two to three seconds to formulate your answer before responding.

Answer not only the questioner but the whole audience. Good presenters tend to maintain eye contact with all the audience, but keep going back to the questioner to check from their body language (e.g., nodding, positive smiling) that they are satisfied with the answer.

Chapter 11 *Questions and Answers* in *English for Presentations at International Conferences*

11.4 What non-technical questions might the audience ask?

Sometimes the audience ask questions that are not specific to your presentation but are related to your research in general.

Look at the questions below. Decide which three you would find the easiest to answer, and which three would be difficult for you. Which one would you most like to be asked?

1. Why did you carry out this research? What gap were you trying to fill?
2. Are there any other research groups working in this area? If so, are their findings similar to yours?
3. What key papers did you read while preparing your research?
4. What did you enjoy most about doing your research?
5. What do you think your key finding was?
6. In your opinion what are the limitations to your research?
7. Could you repeat your main conclusion please?
8. Have you published a paper on this topic?
9. What research are you planning for the future?
10. We are doing similar research. Would it be possible for us to see your full results?

11.5 What if I don't understand a question?

With regard to answering questions:

1. what do you do when you understand nothing at all?
2. when you understand (or think you understand) only a couple of words?
3. when you understand half the question?
4. who should take the responsibility for the fact that you don't understand a question – you or the questioner?

Sometimes the reason you or the audience can't understand the question, is because the questioner is sitting down and he/she cannot be seen or heard very easily. Simply say

Do you think you could stand up and speak a bit louder? Thank you.

This has the added advantage that you have a second chance to hear the question yourself!

Your ability to understand the questions depends not just on you. It is also the responsibility of the questioner to phrase and enunciate the question in a way that you will understand it.

You could say:

Do you think you could ask me that question again during the coffee break?

Would you mind emailing me that question, and then I will get back to you?

Sorry, I really need to check with a colleague before being able to answer that question.

11.5 What if I don't understand a question? (cont.)

If you don't understand a question, particularly from a native speaker of English, it is likely that others in the audience didn't understand either. It is always best to admit to yourself that you will probably not understand the question even if the questioner repeats it. You could say:

> *I am sorry, but like many people in the audience, I am not a native English speaker. Could you speak a little more slowly please? Thank you.*

However, I would avoid asking the questioner to repeat what they said or to speak more slowly. This is because:

- you may be agitated and unable to concentrate as normal
- it will be embarrassing for both of you, and could be a problem if you still don't understand
- the questioner will probably repeat the question in exactly the same way as before, though possibly a little slower – the problem is that native speakers are often not aware that people have problems understanding them
- they may have an accent that is so unfamiliar to you that you will never understand what they have said

If you are really convinced that you will lose face if you do not attempt to answer the question, then see Chapter 9 *What to say when you don't understand what someone has said* in *English for Interacting on Campus*. However, I strongly recommend that you simply ask the questioner to ask you the question during the coffee break. This is the simplest and quickest solution, and it avoids embarrassment for everyone.

See also Chapter 11 (Questions and Answers), *English for Presentations at International Conferences*

Chapter 12
Doing presentations online

12.1 What are the pros and cons of doing presentations online?

1. Would you prefer to <u>see</u> a presentation live at a conference venue or online? Why?
2. Your professor says you have to <u>give</u> a presentation for an international audience. Would you prefer to do it directly at the conference in front a 'real' live audience, or online (again in front of a live audience)? Why?
3. Compared to doing presentations physically in person, what are the typical difficulties of doing presentations online?
4. What are the advantages of doing presentations online rather than in person?

Below are some advantages of online presentations. Which ones do you not agree with and why?

a) You can be in a more relaxing environment.

b) You can read from your script.

c) You can time the presentation almost exactly (although you need to allow for technical difficulties).

d) It is much easier to show slides and highlight particular parts.

e) You are less confined by the colors you can use in your slides in an online presentation as you don't have to worry about how the lighting in the conference room will affect them.

f) The Q&A can be aided by 'chat'.

g) You can use subtitles (4.5).

12.1 What are the pros and cons of doing presentations online? (cont.)

Below are eight possible <u>disadvantages</u> of doing online presentations.

- Did you think of any that are not on this list?
- Which three are the worst and/or most difficult to deal with?
- How can you prevent / avoid the eight disadvantages, or at least mitigate them (i.e. make them less serious)?

1. Technical difficulties in setting up the presentation and wasting time due to bad internet connections.

2. On a laptop your camera is looking up at your face (sometimes up your nose).

3. Audience not in a novel situation, they are sitting in front of their PC like they do every day. No added interest of being in conference venue.

4. The audience has probably watched hundreds of online presentations. Low expectations. You have to work hard not to meet such negative expectations.

5. You can't see your audience as a whole - detached from reality; you can't see if they are nodding, following, losing attention.

6. They only see your face; thus you lose the impact that your body language can give. And because you are static, it is harder for the audience to be involved in what you are saying.

7. Many presenters look down at their notes and thus make no eye contact with audience.

8. More distractions. Audiences are free to look at their phone, write an email, chat to someone else in the room, etc.

12.1 What are the pros and cons of doing presentations online? (cont.)

Below are explanations of how you can avoid the eight problems listed above. The solutions presume that you are using Zoom as your videoconferencing software. But what is said is true of other similar applications.

1) On the days prior to the presentation practise sharing your presentation online and ensure you have a good connection. Make a series of checks via a simulation with friends on Zoom. Connect to Zoom at least 10 minutes before your allocated slot for your presentation so that you can check that your camera comes on and that the audio works.

2) Ensure your camera is not below the height of your eyes.

3, 4) Find new ways of attracting and maintaining their attention (6.3).

5) Ask everyone to keep their video on (see ☼ below), though not everyone will. Choose a group of friendly-looking faces to keep on your screen. Their smiles will boost your confidence.

6) See 12.2 and 12.3.

7) Have your notes directly on your screen or attached to your screen. Have them at eye-level. Consider using a teleprompter: https://demcastusa.com/2020/09/22/communicate-better-on-zoom-keep-eye-contact-with-an-on-screen-teleprompter/

8) Practise making your presentation is as engaging as possible (12.4) - get feedback from colleagues. But don't worry if you catch someone on their phone – it might be something important for them!

Ask your audience to keep their video on. This will enable you to:

- have a sense of the presence of an audience. It is very difficult to talk directly at the screen with no idea of what your audience look like
- see their reactions – it boosts your confidence if you can see people smiling or nodding their heads up and down (this is usually a sign of agreement with what you are saying).

12.2 How important is my appearance?

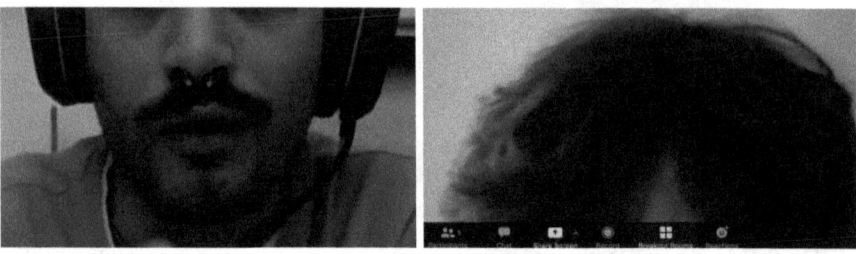

1. What impression do you get from the two photos above? How typical are they in online presentations?
2. In which kind of presentation is your appearance (the way you look) more important: a) online b) in person? Why?
3. Is it acceptable to wear headphones and / or hold your microphone while giving your presentation?
4. What is the best kind of background to have, i.e. what do you want your audiences to see behind you? What kinds of backgrounds do you think are unsuitable?
5. In terms of body language, what should you avoid doing during an online presentation?

Below are some tips related to Zoom and to your appearance.

- Test out all the options available on Zoom (or whatever application you are using) to enhance the way you will physically appear to your audience. All the online meeting software applications have tutorials on how to do this.

- Note that these applications (Microsoft Teams, Webex, Zoom etc.) were originally designed for a business audience. This may explain why they recommend using a mono-color virtual background (generally green – which is apparently less distracting and more professional) or choosing from a series of standard backgrounds. These suggestions are good if you are doing a formal presentation. However, if you want to establish a friendly relationship with your audience, then just have the background of the room where you are. It will make you more authentic and credible.

12.2 How important is my appearance? (cont.)

- Don't do your presentation with headphones (see the photo on the previous page). It makes the audience feel less connected with you.
- Ensure that your clothes are not the same color as your background.
- If you wear glasses, adjust the lighting in your room so that your glasses do not reflect the screen.
- Avoid sitting on a revolving seat, otherwise you will be tempted to move from side to side.
- Don't chew gum.
- Don't play with your hair.

12.3 What about my voice? And body language?

1. Is your voice more important in an online than in person presentation?
2. What kinds of voices inspire you to listen? Do you prefer a 'professional presentation voice' or a friendly voice?
3. What if anything should you do with your hands during an online presentation? What do you need to be careful about?
4. How important are your eyes and where they look?

Be careful of where your hands are: they should NOT be on your head, behind your head, scratching your face, picking your nose, playing with your ear, fiddling with jewelry etc. These things are easy to forget as they tend to be automatic.

Instead try to come keep your hands in front of you and use them to:

- highlight, using your fingers, particular points you are enumerating (e.g. *first, second, third*)
- emphasize the size of something
- show that you are asking a question

Your aim in every presentation is to make a mental and physical connection with the audience. In an 'online' presentation look towards the middle to upper part of the computer screen. Don't move your head much, but change the direction of your eyes. In an 'in person' presentation move your head and eyes so that you can look at everyone in the audience (13.2). If you look at members of the audience, they feel more involved and thus more willing to listen to you.

If you have prepared a printed script (Chapter 3) of what you are going to say, then avoid looking down on your desk to be able to read it. There are several solutions:

- incorporate your script into your presentation file
- upload the script onto your desktop so that it is very close to the presentation
- use sticky tape to stick the script physically onto the screen

All these solutions enable you to maintain eye contact with your audience.

12.4 How can I gain and keep audience attention online?

1. Why is it important to have the audience's attention right at the beginning of your presentation? If you don't get their attention, what might happen?
2. In an in-person presentation, what techniques can you use to gain their attention? (Chapter 6)
3. Which of the techniques from an in-person presentation can you apply to an online presentation?
4. What additional techniques can you use in an online presentation?

In one sense, getting attention online is easy. You share your presentation and suddenly it appears on the audience's screen. So they should be motivated at least to look at the title slide!

However, it is difficult to maintain the audience's attention. This is for obvious reasons. The audience:

- are not in a novel situation, they are sitting in front of their PC like they do every day – there is not the added interest of being in a conference hall
- have probably watched hundreds of online presentations, and their expectations are likely to be low – so you have to work hard not to meet such negative expectations
- have many more distractions, and are much freer to look at their phone, write an email, chat to someone else in the room, etc.
- can only see your face, thus you lose the impact that your body language can give

So what can you do? What strategies can / do you use to attract and maintain audience attention?

12.4 How can I gain and keep audience attention online? (cont.)

Look at the list below. Which points refer to gaining (G) attention, and which ones to maintaining (M) attention throughout your presentation? In some cases you can put both G and M.

1. Look at camera (not down at your notes).
2. Talk like you're talking to a good friend.
3. Be enthusiastic.
4. Prepare visually easy-to-follow, pleasing, and varied slides.
5. Give clear explanations.
6. Give interesting statistics.
7. Use a striking video / photo / image that the audience have probably never seen before.
8. Tell a personal story.
9. Say something about the country where you come from.
10. Ask the audience a question.
11. Give an example before explaining the theory.
12. Keep it short and simple (KISS).
13. Emphasize key words.
14. Seem and sound friendly and empathetic.
15. Don't make the audience feel stupid.
16. Make the first slide and last slide visually similar to create a sense of completion.

Typically 7, 8, 9 and 10 are used to attract audience attention at the beginning of a presentation. Also, 1, 6 and 15 may be particularly relevant at the beginning. The others are useful for maintaining attention.

12.5 How can I have minimal text / diagrams in my slides, but also enable my audience to access a very detailed version of my presentation?

1. Which do you prefer in an online presentation, slides that are full of text and graphs OR slides with minimal text and graphs? Why?
2. How could you achieve both objectives, e.g. both full text AND minimal text at the same time?

1) If you have a lot of text or diagrams (and animations), this means that you will have to talk about the same slide for a long time. A long time in a presentation is anything more than 20 seconds. If you want to keep your audience's attention you need to change slides frequently. This also enables to you to produce more slides with less information on each slide, so that the slide is easy to talk about.

2) In an online presentation, in theory the audience could see two versions of your presentation at the same time.

- In the 'minimal' version, which is the one that you will be presenting, there is a reduced number of texts, graphs and other images.
- In the 'detailed' version, which you can email them beforehand, you can have the same slides in the same order, but in much more detail.
- You can also have additional slides, which can refer to when necessary, e.g. to answer a question during the Q&A session.

Those members of your online audience who cannot follow what you are saying – maybe their level of English is low or maybe your accent is very unfamiliar – can follow on the detailed slides.

Alternatively, if you haven't given your audience your detailed slides, after your presentation you can say: *If you need to find out more details, then please refer to the other version of the slides that I emailed you. Of course, if you have any further questions, you can email me at my address which is shown on last slide.*

12.6 Should my slides be different just because I am online?

Make sure your audience can only see the slide that you are talking about (first image below), rather than the current slide AND the next slide (second image). Clearly, if they have downloaded the detailed version mentioned in 12.5, you cannot control what they are looking at.

AUDIENCE SHOULD SEE THIS

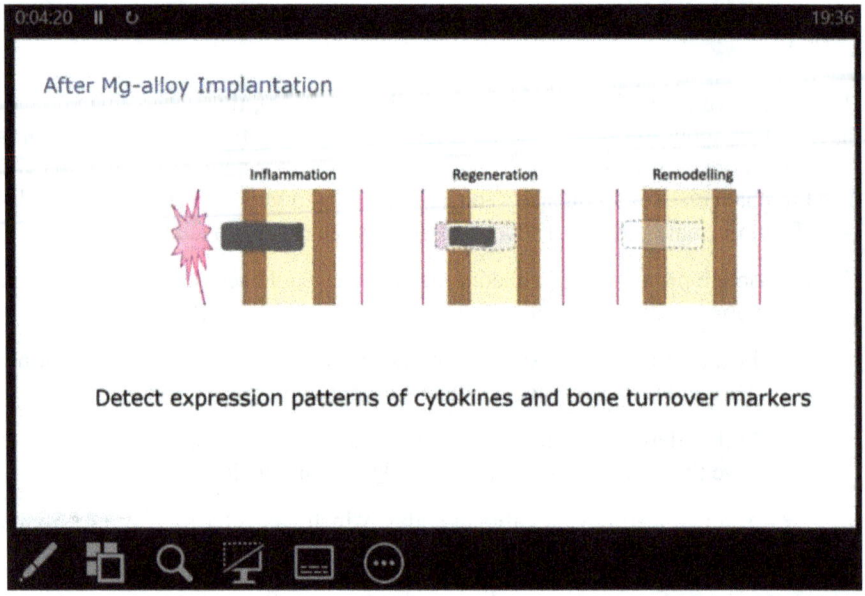

12.6 Should my slides be different just because I am online? (cont.)

AUDIENCE SHOULD NOT SEE THIS

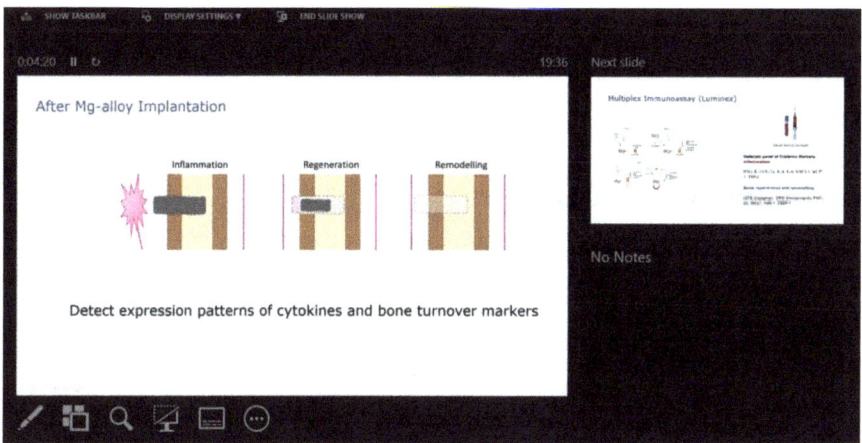

The more the audience can see, the more they will be distracted. Their curiosity will certainly mean that they start reading the next slide while you are still discussing the first slide.

For more details on what the audience should and should not see: 13.3.

Also, make sure your 'Notes' are hidden.

In theory, in online conference presentations, your slides can be fuller because your face is probably smaller, so the audience is not focusing on your 'photo' but on your slides and what you say.

12.7 Where can I find tips for using Zoom to help me improve my online presentations?

How good are you from a technical point of view at using online presentation programs?

Which of the following do you know how to do? Which ones do you think are the most useful?

1. Create a virtual background
2. Set up a green screen for a virtual background
3. Touch up your appearance
4. Transcribe your presentation
5. Share multiple windows
6. Write on the whiteboard
7. Use the annotation tools

Watch this expert - Kevin Stratvert - explaining how to use features outlined in 1-7 above, plus many others.

> https://www.youtube.com/watch?v=UEABW3ddZkc

Note Kevin talks for about 20 minutes - skip the parts that you are not interested in. However, if you do have time, Kevin shares a lot of tips to solve problems that you didn't even know you had!!

Which two of his tips did you find the most useful?

There are a lot of experts on YouTube who give technical tips regarding Zoom. One that I found particularly useful is this one created by Scott Friesen (thank you Scott!):

> https://www.youtube.com/watch?v=25Awq_v1Zms

There are three tips that I think you should check out. The times are the moments these tips appear in the video.

12.7 Where can I find tips for using Zoom to help me improve my online presentations? (cont.)

0.29 keyboard shortcuts for sharing screen

If you can't find Zoom's 'share' button - maybe because you have other windows covering it - simply press Alt + S on your PC. Of if you have a Mac: command + shift + S.

4.00 optimizing the video quality when sharing videos

Scott shows a relatively little-used feature that will mean that your audience will be able to see better any videos that you show or have incorporated into your presentation.

5.00 just sharing a portion of your screen

For me, this is this is the most useful tip. Scott shows you how to show just specific parts of your screen rather than your entire desktop. This means that you can share your presentation AND have other files and programs open on your desktop.

12.8 What if I have problems connecting and my audience can only hear me but not see my presentation?

If you are worried that you might have a technical fault and be unable to share your presentation, then a good solution is to email the participants the presentation beforehand.

During the presentation you will then need to tell them which slide you are talking about. For example: ... *and the results showed that x=y. Next slide / Slide 22 So on the basis that x=y, we then ...*

12.9 What are the typical mistakes of online presentations?

What don't you like about other people's online presentations? Think about the presentations that you have seen

- given by your colleagues, fellow students, lecturers and professors
- while participating in an online conference (or watching a pre-recorded one)

On the next page is a list of DON'TS, i,e. things that one expert recommends that you should NOT do when giving presentations.

- Which ones i) refer exclusively to online (O) presentations, ii) refer exclusively to face-to-face live (L) presentations, and iii) which to all (A) types of presentations (online and live)?
- Which ones do you NOT agree with? Why?

12.9 What are the typical mistakes of online presentations? (cont.)

DO NOT

1. Expect your audience to read your slides at the same time as you are explaining them.
2. Give too much information.
3. Go: *um, er, erm, ah*.
4. Have crowded slides.
5. Have slides full of text.
6. Hold the microphone in your hand.
7. Introduce yourself or your department.
8. Look down.
9. Pace incessantly from one side of the stage to the other.
10. Read your title.
11. Say *OK?* at the end of every sentence.
12. Speak too fast.
13. Spend too long on the same slide.
14. Talk too much (i.e. no real pauses).
15. Touch any part of your face.
16. Touch your jewelry, or click your pen.
17. Use animations.
18. Use your hands and arms too frequently.
19. Wear headphones.
20. Have a last slide that simply says: 'Thank you for your attention'.

Source: *2000 tips for a memorable and captivating presentation* by Frank O. Pinion

O: 6, 15, 19
L: 9, 15, 18
A: all the others

Chapter 13
Practising, improving, and getting feedback

13.1 How should I revise my slides?

Practise your presentation several times. Identify any slides or parts of your speech that:

- need to be simplified
- could be cut

The main aim of a presentation is to arouse an audience's curiosity and to stimulate their desire for more information.

A presentation is like the trailer to a movie – you only see (hear) the highlights. This then stimulates your desire to watch the whole movie to get the complete picture, or in the case of a presentation to read the relevant paper/documentation.

Look at your slides and check that they:

- will gain the audience's attention
- are in the best order (use the 'slide sorter' option to move them around – see 9.1)
- do not all look the same (you need to have some visual variety)
- really support the objective of your presentation
- are clear and simple

You will certainly know much more about the topic than your audience needs to know. But you only need to tell them two or three key points – don't try to pack in too much information.

13.1 How should I revise my slides? (cont.)

To help you decide what to include, imagine that the length of your allocated time for the presentation was reduced, for example, from 20 mins to 10 mins. Decide which points

- the audience might already know or not be interested in
- you have included simply because you think you SHOULD include them, because you think it is more professional to cover everything or because you think by putting them in you will make a good impression on your boss
- you have included simply because you yourself find them interesting but they are in fact not particularly relevant
- could be grouped together under one category so that they could be covered together and more quickly

Chapter 15 *Rehearsing and Self-assessment* in *English for Presenting at International Conferences.*

13.2 What should I focus on while practising / rehearsing my presentation?

Offline and Online

PRACTISE EXACTLY WHAT YOU ARE GOING TO SAY

If you have not written a script (Chapter 3) and / or have not practised what you are going to say, your presentation is likely to be full of redundancy.

VARY THE PARTS YOU PRACTISE

You may only have time to practice part of your presentation at a single time. The result may be that you only practice the first half of your presentation. Occasionally begin in the middle, or begin with the conclusions - don't just focus on the beginning and the technical part.

PREPARE FOR FORGETTING WHAT YOU WANT TO SAY

A frequent problem is forgetting a specific word or phrase that you need to say.

There are three good solutions for this, you can:

- look at your notes (either on your laptop or phone, or on a printed sheet)
- drink some water, or take out a tissue to wipe your nose, and use this time to remind yourself
- say *I am sorry I can't think of the word. In any case* ... And then you simply proceed with the next pointPREPARE FOR THE PREVIOUS PRESENTATION GOING OVER THE ALLOCATED TIME

You may have an unexpected time restriction due to previous presenters not respecting their time slots. Prepare for this by:

- knowing exactly how much time you need for each part of your presentation
- having your most important points near the beginning of the presentation, never just in the second half
- thinking in advance what slides you could cut, particularly those in the latter part of the presentation
- planning how to reduce the amount you say for particular slides
- using options in your presentation software that allow you to skip slides

13.2 What should I focus on while practising / rehearsing my presentation? (cont.)

PRACTICE ANSWERING QUESTIONS

Imagine the question, and then answer it in various ways (including imagining that you didn't understand the question) – see 11.5.

PREPARE FOR TECHNICAL DISASTERS

Typical problems: your presentation won't upload, you can't share it, it freezes, you lose connection. The best solution is to be able to do your presentation without slides. And if you practise your presentation without any slides, you will learn that i) it is possible to do a presentation with no slides, ii) some of your slides are redundant or misleading, so you can cut or replace them.

ASK COLLEAGUES TO CHECK YOUR PRESENTATION

Make sure that your colleagues see your presentation before you actually present it at the conference. Email them the presentation beforehand so that they can make suggestions and also so that they will then know what to expect. If your colleagues have not seen the presentation and watch it for the first time at the conference, they may be really pleased with what you have done or they may react in a negative way that undermines your confidence.

Ask someone who has never seen your presentation to check the spelling. If you check the spelling just by yourself, you will be unlikely to spot mistakes. We generally see what we think we have written rather than what is actually written.

Offline only

SIMULATE TALKING TO YOUR AUDIENCE

Stand at one end of the biggest room of your house. Imagine that the pieces of furniture (chairs, tables, desks, shelves, even windows) in various parts of the room are members of the audience. Practice talking to each item. Spend no more than two seconds on each piece of furniture, then move on to another piece.

SIMULATE HAVING A SCREEN BEHIND YOU

Imagine the screen is behind you. Think about the best place to stand. If you stand in front of the screen, the beam will light you up and audience won't really be able to see you. To avoid blocking your slides from the audience's view, stand to one side of the screen. Only move in front of it when it is strictly necessary to point to things on your slides.

Note that if you stand on the left side of the screen, you will probably focus just on those members of the audience on the right-hand side (and vice versa). So you need to keep swapping sides.

13.2 What should I focus on while practising / rehearsing my presentation? (cont.)

STAND UP AND MOVE AROUND

Do not to sit and talk into your laptop. When you are sitting, your voice does not project as well as it does when you are standing.

If you move in a relaxed, but not repetitive, manner in front of the audience, it will give them the impression that you are at ease and comfortable in the presentation environment. And by implication your ease will make the audience think you are confident about your presentation itself.

THINK ABOUT WHAT YOU WILL DO WITH YOUR HANDS

Do whatever comes most naturally to you with your hands and arms. Inexperienced presenters often begin by rigidly holding their arms to their side, or folding them across their chest. Such positions tend to make the audience feel that you are nervous or may be a bit hostile.

Overcome your nervousness by holding something in your hand, for instance a pointer or a pen. Try only to do this for a few minutes, as it stops you making full use of your hands.

13.3 What should I focus on in the days before an online presentation?

It is imperative that you practise uploading and sharing your presentation while on Zoom, Teams etc. – it is very frustrating for the audience to see you frantically trying to share your presentation.

You do NOT want your audience to see your presentation in the format below:

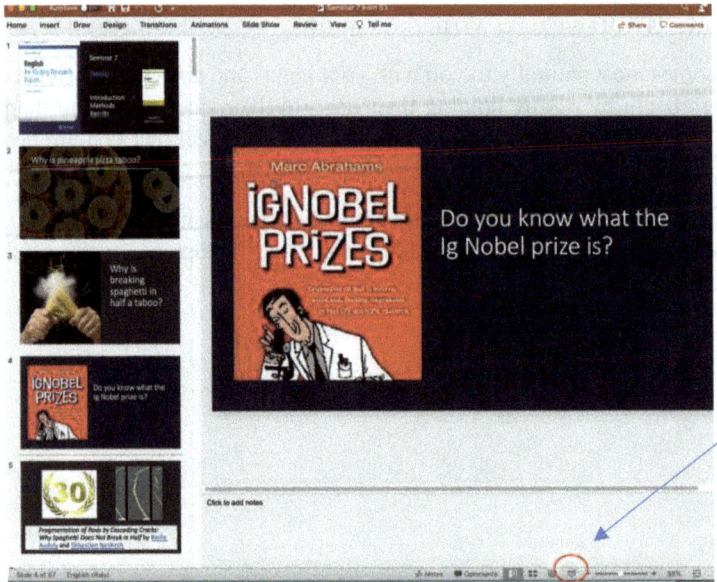

You want the audience just to see the <u>main slide</u>, not the other slides. You can achieve this by hitting the button highlighted in the above slide at the bottom left with a red circle (see the end of the arrow). The audience will just see the image below:

13.3 What should I focus on in the days before an online presentation? (cont.)

The viewing option shown in the screenshot below works for an in-person conference, but NOT online. If you are doing your presentation online and you want to see your other slides, a good option is to print them in slide sorter option.

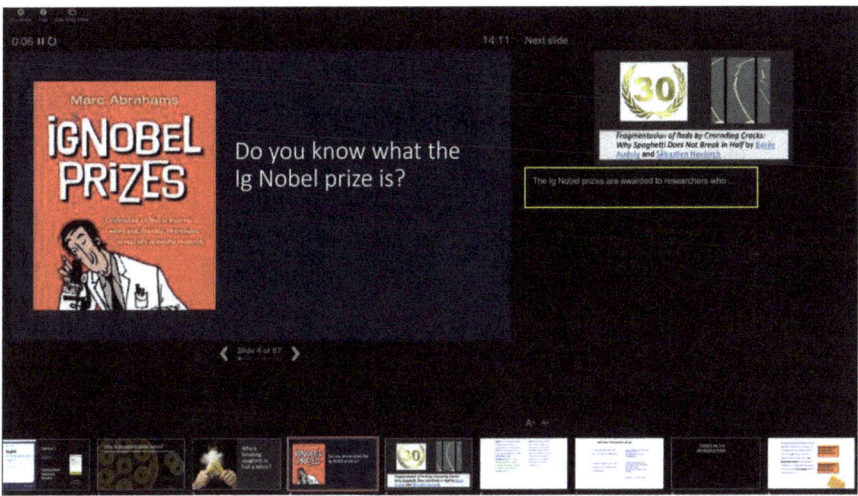

With viewing option shown in the screenshot above, the audience only sees the main slide, but YOU can see <u>everything</u>:

- the main slide
- the next slide
- your script / notes (in the image I have highlighted these with a yellow rectangle)
- where you are in your presentation by looking at the bar at the bottom

You can get this view option in PowerPoint by selecting Slide Show (towards the right of the menu bar) and then clicking on Presenter View.

13.3 What should I focus on in the days before an online presentation? (cont.)

Note: The screenshots show the cover *Ignobel Prizes* by Marc Abrahams. For details about the Ignobel Prizes see www.improbable.com where you will find a lot of very interesting non-mainstream research.

Note: This solution means that you CANNOT see anything else on your desktop. To learn how to view a PowerPoint presentation without using a full screen, see this very useful guide:

https://ito-engineering.screenstepslive.com/s/ito_fase/m/94256/l/1243152-how-can-i-view-a-powerpoint-show-without-using-full-screen

Also, ensure you check that your face is central and close. The more of a 'connection' you will create with them. Obviously you don't want to position your face 2 cm from the camera, but about 20-30 cm is a good distance. Check that your voice is clear and that your microphone isn't moving around (this makes an unpleasant noise for the audience).

All these issues are quite simple to control when you are practising, but remember when you are nervous you might inadvertently hit the wrong button. This is why it is crucial to practise again and again, preferably with an audience of friends or colleagues.

13.4 How can I improve my presentation skills?

LEARN HOW TO GAIN AND KEEP YOUR AUDIENCE'S ATTENTION

Below are some good ways of attracting and holding your audience's attention:

1. have a clear idea who your audience are, don't assume that they are naturally going to be interested in your topic
2. have an agenda and a clear structure with clear transitions so that the audience know where you are going
3. have clear transitions from one slide to another to make it easy for the audience to follow what you are saying
4. help the audience to understand why you are showing them a particular slide
5. involve your audience and give them lots of examples
6. make frequent eye contact
7. avoid too much text on your slides
8. use simple graphs and tables
9. make your text and visuals big enough for everyone in the audience to see clearly
10. avoid entering into too much detail (i.e. just select those things that the audience really need to know about the topic)
11. avoid spending more than a couple of minutes on one specific detail
12. have a variety of types of slides (not just all bullets, or all text, or all photos)
13. speak reasonably slowly and move from slide to slide at a speed that the audience will feel comfortable with
14. vary your tone of voice
15. occasionally stop talking for five seconds or more

EXPLOIT MOMENTS OF HIGH AUDIENCE ATTENTION

Audiences tend to remember things that are said at the beginning and end of a presentation, because their attention is generally higher at these points.

They also remember things that they hear more than once.

And finally they remember curious facts, i.e. things that stand out.

13.4 How can I improve my presentation skills? (cont.)

Ideally you need to state your key points both at the beginning and ending. In the middle go through each key point more in detail. If possible, include an unexpected / counterintuitive / interesting fact for each key point.

DON'T TELL THE AUDIENCE EVERYTHING YOU KNOW, ONLY WHAT THEY NEED TO KNOW

Try to avoid the temptation to give the audience the full Wikipedia explanation. When you've written out your speech (Chapter 3) for the first time, revise it, and if possible, reduce the amount you have written.

Don't state the obvious. If your slide is entitled 'Roadmap' and shows a list of milestones that have already been done and things that will be done in the future. Don't say:

> This is a roadmap of the XXX project. We have already achieved the first two steps and we now have a beta version with full functionality. The plan is to have final version next year.

Instead just point to the relevant parts of the slide and say:

> This is what we've done already, and the plan is to have the final version early next year.

So don't refer to things that are clear from the slide and need no further explanation.

AVOID DETAILS / EXCEPTIONS ETC

Don't think that you have to include all the details because this is what your prof, colleagues or the audience expect of you. You may think that by leaving them out, you will be considered to be unprofessional or worse not to know about your job.

However, if you give all the details, you will force your audience 1) to hear extremely complex explanations that cover all possible cases, and 2) to look at extremely complex tables and graphs.

Don't worry about leaving out the details. Just introduce what you say with a qualification:

> This is an extremely simplified view of the situation, but it is enough to illustrate that ...

> In reality this table should also include other factors, but for the sake of simplicity I have just chosen these two key points:

> Broadly speaking, I think we can say that ...

13.4 How can I improve my presentation skills? (cont.)

You can then tell the audience that the details are provided in your paper, on your online profile, or on the conference website where you have uploaded a more detailed presentation (see 8.2 and 12.5).

DON'T SPEND TOO LONG ON ONE SLIDE

We can only look at something static for about 30 seconds and then we start thinking about something else. So if possible, reduce the amount of time you spend showing the same slide.

REPEAT KEY WORDS AND CONCEPTS FREQUENTLY

Don't be afraid to make the same point twice, but try and express it in a different way. For example, if you are telling people how to make money, you can re-explain the concept in terms of how not to lose money.

This will enable your audience to:

- follow what you are saying better,
- catch concepts the second time if they missed them the first time
- remember afterwards what you have said

If you use a non-technical word which you think the audience may not know, say it and then paraphrase it. Example: *These devices are tiny; they are very small*.

Parts of this section were taken from *Presentations, Demos, and Training Sessions* which is part of a non-academic series called *Guides to Professional English* (published by SpringerNature). You might find this book useful if you move from research to industry and need to make a presentation for your company.

13.5 How easy is it to judge one's own performance?

1. List three weak points that you have when giving a presentation.
2. If you asked your colleagues for feedback on your presentations, do you think they would notice the same weak points as you listed above?
3. What typical weak points do your colleagues have? Do you think they would agree with your assessment?
4. If you were with a group of colleagues and you were assessing the presentation of another colleague, do you think as a group you would be unanimous in your assessment?

Many non-native English-speaking presenters do not have a clear idea of what their weak points are, but presume (imagine) that they are connected i) to their level of English:

- grammatical and vocabulary mistakes
- poor pronunciation and intonation

and ii) to anxiety / nerves.

In reality their problems tend not to be language-related, and frequently have nothing to do with their nerves. For example, they fail to notice that:

- they spent much of the presentation with their back to the audience (i.e. at an in-person conference)
- when they were actually facing the audience, they weren't looking at them directly, but either above their heads or towards the ground
- there was too much text in their slides
- that they made distracting *um* or *er* sounds between one slide and another
- they showed little enthusiasm
- etc. (see 1.3 for a list of other typical defects)

Basically, we are not good at assessing our weaknesses (and strengths!), but very good at assessing those of others! So, before doing a presentation at a conference, always present in front of your friends and colleagues and ask for their feedback.

13.6 How should I ask for feedback while preparing my presentation?

1. In what areas of your life do people tend to give you feedback on? a) school and university work, b) performance at work, c) performance at sports, arts etc.

2. Typically, why are people reluctant to give others (outside their family) feedback on: a) their behavior, b) their voice, c) the way they look, d) their voice, e) the length of time they spend talking, ... ?

3. What kind of feedback would be useful for someone who has just done their presentation online? What particular aspects of an online presentation can we give feedback on? Are some of these aspects different from an in-person presentation?

It is very difficult to judge your own performance with regard to how well you have delivered your presentation. Also, people tend not to offer feedback, even if they know it could help you. This means that you need to specifically ask for feedback. But you are unlikely to learn anything useful if you simply ask people: *So, what did you think of my presentation?* or *Can you give me some feedback on my presentation?*

Instead you need to give them a checklist of things to think about. Try using the following assessment sheet:

13.6 How should I ask for feedback while preparing my presentation? (cont.)

Assessment Sheet

FIRST SLIDES AND AUDIENCE INVOLVEMENT

- ☐ Attention of audience immediately gained
- ☐ Topic clearly related to audience
- ☐ Audience personally involved in some way
- ☐ Variety to maintain attention

STRUCTURE

- ☐ Strong beginning - topic introduced clearly
- ☐ Overall topic previewed
- ☐ Clear transitions and links between points
- ☐ Clear conclusions and strong ending

SLIDES

- ☐ Clear text
- ☐ Simple diagrams
- ☐ Not too much detail
- ☐ No distracting colors, fonts, animations

BODY LANGUAGE

- ☐ Eyes directed to audience
- ☐ Moved around (in-person only)
- ☐ Used hands appropriately

VOICE / DELIVERY

- ☐ Right speed - did not begin in a rush
- ☐ Clear and loud voice
- ☐ Short clear phrases, individual words articulated clearly
- ☐ No annoying noises (*er, erm, um*)
- ☐ Good pronunciation
- ☐ Good English (grammar, vocab)
- ☐ Enthusiastic and friendly
- ☐ Sounded credible

FINAL SLIDE

- ☐ Clear reasons for contacting presenter
- ☐ Memorable
- ☐ Approachable

13.7 What will I learn if I make a video of me doing my presentation?

If you are embarrassed to ask for feedback, video yourself. When your replay the video, check that you do:

- not look at the screen, ceiling or floor instead of making eye contact with the audience
- not make hand gestures that might be considered irritating, repetitive or inappropriate
- not inadvertently touch inappropriate parts of your body
- not make distracting sounds: *um, erm, er* etc.

13.8 How can I get feedback automatically when rehearsing?

Rehearse is another word for *practise*.

Microsoft PowerPoint has a useful option called 'Rehearse with Coach' which you will find under the 'Slide Show' menu.

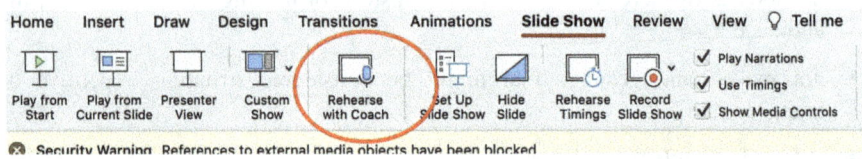

Click on 'Rehearse with Coach', then practise doing your presentation (or part of it). Make sure you are on full screen. PowerPoint then gives you a commentary in real time (i.e. while you are doing the presentation) or presents a report when you have finished – see screenshot below.

> **Fillers**: these are words such as *you know*, *I mean* or *OK?*, or sounds such as *em, erm, er, ah*.
>
> **Inclusiveness**: ensures you don't use any insensitive language.
>
> **Pace**: how fast you speak.
>
> **Pitch**: variation in your intonation.
>
> **Originality**: whether you simply read the text from the slides or not.

Press the 'Learn More' buttons to get a useful document entitled 'Suggestions from Presenter Coach'.

13.8 How can I get feedback automatically when rehearsing? (cont.)

When you've finished rehearsing, PowerPoint generates the report below:

Chapter 15 *Rehearsing and Self-assessment* in *English for Presenting at International Conferences.*

Aims of this book

WHO FOR

- Intermediate to upper intermediate students of academic English
- EAP teachers

TYPE

Self-study guide for students, as well as the basis for a course on academic English.

STRUCTURE OF BOOK

Each chapter covers a specific area of giving presentations, from preparing a script and slides, to giving the presentation (online or at a traditional conference).

STRUCTURE OF CHAPTERS

Each chapter is made up of a series of sections. Most sections begin with a series of questions to get students thinking about the big picture of a specific area of presenting or communicating in general. Then there are explanations and key tips, as well as a series of short exercises.

Other books in this series

Like this Giving Presentations book, the two books below are also aimed at students with an intermediate level or above.

Writing an Academic Paper in English: Intermediate Level

Essential English Grammar and Communication Strategies: Intermediate Level

The other books in The 'English for Academic' series also includes the following books, which can be integrated into a course on English for Academic Purposes (EAP).

English for Writing Research Papers

English for Presentations at International Conferences

English for Research: Usage, Style, and Grammar

100 Tips to Avoid Mistakes in Academic Writing and Presenting

English for Academic Research: Writing Exercises

English for Academic Research: Grammar Writing Exercises

English for Academic Research: Vocabulary Writing Exercises

English for Academic Correspondence

English for Interacting on Campus

English for Academic CVs, Resumes, and Online Profiles

For details see: https://www.springer.com/series/13913.

Icons

  Explanation of a rule / guideline.

   Have discussion or think about.

  Expert tips.

  An exercise to do.

  Key to the discussion points or exercise.

  Books in the *English for Research* series where readers can find extra details and/or exercises.

How this book differs from *English for Presentations at International Conferences*

This is the second book I have published with SpringerNature on how to give presentations. The one you are reading now can be used as coursebook or as a self-study guide. It is a very practical book. I had a lot of fun writing it, so I hope you have fun using it!

The other book – *English for Presentations at International Conferences* – is more like a manual. It covers several areas that are not covered in the book you are reading now. It includes chapters on: ten ways to begin a presentation (Chapter 6), talking about the methodology (8), discussing results (9), attracting and keeping audience attention (12), rehearsing and self-assessment (15), networking (16, 17), posters (18), useful phrases (20). It is intended for a more advanced reader.

FOR EAP TEACHERS: RATIONALE BEHIND THE BOOK AND HOW TO USE IT

ENGLISH LEVEL OF STUDENTS

This book is intended to teach students how to prepare and present their research at conferences. This presupposes that the students will be Master's, PhDs or post-grad students. In my experience of teaching international students, most of them have reached at least a mid-upper intermediate level of English (CEFR B2), and many of them will be at a very advanced level. This book is aimed at <u>all</u> those students, so it can be used with mid intermediate students to advanced students – and such students can all be part of the same class. In fact, many of the skills taught in this book are language independent, they are much more about communication. The guidelines given will often work for the student's native language too.

STRUCTURE

Each chapter is independent of the other chapters. This means, for example, that you don't have to have covered Chapters 1-3 in order to do Chapter 4. So this is not a conventional coursebook where you start at Unit 1 and finish at Unit 10.

The structure of a typical chapter is:

- A discussion on the importance of the topic covered by the chapter. For example, Chapter 4 is on pronunciation and intonation. So the initial discussion is on why pronunciation is a key part of giving a good presentation.
- Then each subsection deals with a different aspect of the main topic. The focus is on students learning practical ideas that are easy to implement immediately.
- Some sections contain short exercises to practise a particular aspect of the main topic.
- Each subsection also contains various tips and explanations.

The subsections are in a logical order and tend to be in order of importance. However, you are free to change the order in which you cover the subsections and to leave out those subsections that you feel are less important for your particular students, or which you simply don't have time to do.

ENCOURAGING STUDENTS TO REVIEW EACH OTHER'S WORK

Encourage your students to work together when preparing their presentations. It is not important if they are from different disciplines – the aim of a presentation is generally the same and the techniques for getting a message across do not (or perhaps should not) differ from discipline to discipline.

Often we are better at seeing the defects and possible improvements in other people's work rather than our own. Giving feedback is also a key skill for an academic as they are likely to be called on to review a co-author's work, to do peer reviews for journals, or to respond to feedback on their own paper in their rebuttal letter. So if you can teach students how to give diplomatic feedback you will be teaching them a real life skill.

HOW TO APPROACH AND TEACH EACH CHAPTER

Let's take Chapter 6 'Starting Your Presentation' as an example.

1. Before teaching this course you need to be really clear what the aim of a presentation is - see Chapter 1 in this book and also Chapter 1 in *English for Presentations at International Conferences*.

2. Go on YouTube and ted.com to see how researchers and 'experts' begin their presentations. Try to find examples of academic presentations. PhD students often partake in competitions, typically known as 3-minute presentations – there are lots of these on YouTube, and the winners generally have a very good technique for starting their presentation.

3. Read through Chapter 6 in this book, and decide which subsections you feel are the most important, and any that you could skip.

4. Look at the exercises, particularly the ones marked 💬 or 💬. These are discussion exercises (both icons mean the same thing), with a series of questions to answers, which involve students working in pairs or groups. However, if you wish, rather than using them as oral exercises, students can simply write the answers. In any case, I recommend using them as oral exercises in order to create variety in your lessons.

5. Now decide the best order to do your chosen subsections and exercises. Note that most subsections are independent of each other, so you don't have to follow the order presented in the book.

6. Prepare a few notes for your lesson plan and then you're ready to go! Don't worry if you don't follow your lesson plan, let the students' needs, interests and curiosity dictate what you cover.

HOW LONG SHOULD IT TAKE TO TEACH EACH CHAPTER?

Each chapter should take 2-4 hours. The time taken will depend on how experienced you are as an EAP teacher, how many subsections you decide to cover, and how many exercises are set for homework rather than being done in class.

I would say you need a minimum of 20 hours to complete a course. In those 20 hours you will not be able to cover all the points in the book, but certainly the most important ones. However, you could extend it to 40, 60 or even 90 hours if you i) did all the exercises, and ii) combined it with a course on giving papers: see the companion volume *How to write an academic paper - a coursebook*. There are many common skills between writing and presenting, so students will have a much clearer and more practical idea of how to implement these skills in a combined course.

SHOULD THE STUDENTS PRODUCE A PRESENTATION AS THEY GO THROUGH THE BOOK?

I suggest that you do NOT get students to produce an entirely new presentation from scratch. It is much more practical for students to look at presentations they have already made and re-work them. My method is to get students to email me a presentation and then:

1. I show two or three slides of two or three of their presentations to highlight issues that I think the presentations have in relation to the part of the presentation that we are currently discussing in our lessons.

2. I then ask everyone to revise for homework two or three slides of their presentation.

3. In the next lesson, either in pairs or in front of the whole class, the students show their three slides. As a class we then comment on the slides.

4. If necessary, students then repeat steps 2 and 3, or move on to a different part of their presentation.

On the other hand, starting from scratch adds a considerable burden to the students' already heavy workload. If they don't have a presentation, they could use one of their tutors' presentations or a fellow student's.

EXAMPLE OF A FULL PRESENTATION GIVEN BY A PHD STUDENT

On my website (e4ac.com/resources) you can find a complete presentation, with slides and script. This downloadable pdf contains my comments on why I believe it is such an effective presentation and why it reflects the guidelines in this book.

TEACHER'S BOOK ON EAP

If you are interested in learning about EAP teaching in general, then you can read *English for Academic Research: A guide for teachers*. This teacher's book gives you a lot of background information on academia and the importance of publishing papers and presenting research at conferences. It was written before the book you are reading now, so it makes no reference to this new series.

About the Author

Adrian Wallwork is the co-founder of English for Academics (e4ac.com), which specializes in editing and revising scientific papers, as well as teaching English as a foreign language to PhD students. He has written course books for Oxford University Press, discussion books for Cambridge University Press, and other books for BEP and Scholastic and several publishers in Italy. He also self publishes discussion books (tefldiscussions.com).

For SpringerNature, he has written three series of books on Academic English, Business English and General English.

His passion is teaching PhD students and researchers how to write and present their research – see https://e4ac.com/courses

Acknowledgements

Biggest thanks, as always, to Anna Southern my unofficial editor. And thanks to Susan Safren at Springer for believing in this project.

Thank you Myriam Capula for producing a superb presentation.

A huge thanks to the following PhD students who gave me permission to reproduce their slides:

Eva Maria Gomez Alvarez, Akash Deep Biswas, Francesco Barbieri, Mario Bernardi, Sabrina Ciancia, Lorenzo della Maggiora, Davide De Luca, Amerigo Ferrari, Alberto Francia, Valerio Ianniciello, Veronica La Rocca, Vittoria Marsili, Valentina Rustichini, Laura Sommovigo, Min Soe Thein, Sonali Verma, Agata Zamborlin

Thank you to Willemijn Doedens and Frob Duguid, whose 3-minute thesis presentations I found on YouTube but who I was unable to contact.

Thanks to Matteo Berton for his illustration, and to Marc Abrahams for allowing me to reproduce the cover of his wonderful book *Ignobel Prizes*.

Thank you to Joaquín Tintoré, whose paper inspired the first subsection of this book.

I would also like to thank TED talks for giving me permission to quote from Jay Walker's presentation.

Feedback welcomed

If you have any feedback on this or any of my other books: adrian.wallwork@gmail.com

Index

A
accent, 4.3
agenda, 7
appearance, 12.2
attention, keeping, 6, 12.4

B
beginning your presentation, 6
big picture, 6.1, 7.5
body language, 12.3
bullet points, 6.8, 8.4, 8.5

C
cartoons, 9.6
conclusions, 10.1, 10.2
contact details, getting audience to contact you, 10.4
country, talking about your, 6.6

D
design ideas (ppt), 9.4
detail, dealing with, 8.2, 12.5
dislikes about other people's presentations, 1.3
displaying your slides to the audience, 12.6, 13.2

F
fears, 1.5
feedback, 13.6, 13.8

final slides, 10
first impressions, 1.6
first slides, 5.5, 6
font and format for editing script, 3.7

G
Google Translate, 3.8
graphs, 8.3

H
headers, 9.3
humanities/arts presentations, 1.8, 5.4
humor, 9.6, 9.7

I
images, 5.3 (in titles), 9
intonation, 4
introductions, 6.8, 6.9

L
limitations, discussing, 10.5

M
memorable, being, 1.7

O
online presentations, 12

P
PhD presentations on YouTube, 2.7
practising, 13
pronunciation, 4

Q
Q&A session, 11
questions, asking audience, 6.4

R
rehearsing, 13
resources online, 2
restrictions on the number of slides, 9.8

S
scripts, 3
skills needed to be an academic, 1.1
slide sorter, 9.1
slide titles, 9.3
software, 12.7
speaking slowly and clearly, 2.5
starting your presentation, 6
statistics, 8.5–8.9
subtitling your presentation, 4.5

T
technical slides, 8
TED, 2, 3.4
text, reducing number of words, 9.2
tips online on how to give a good presentation, 2.6
title slides, 5
two versions of your presentation, 8.2, 12.5

U
understanding questions, 11.5

V
videoing yourself, 13.7
voice, 12.3

Y
YouTube, 2.7

Z
Zoom tips, 12.7

GPSR Compliance
The European Union's (EU) General Product Safety Regulation (GPSR) is a set of rules that requires consumer products to be safe and our obligations to ensure this.

If you have any concerns about our products, you can contact us on

ProductSafety@springernature.com

In case Publisher is established outside the EU, the EU authorized representative is:

Springer Nature Customer Service Center GmbH
Europaplatz 3
69115 Heidelberg, Germany

www.ingramcontent.com/pod-product-compliance
Lightning Source LLC
LaVergne TN
LVHW050144270326
834688LV00077B/787